Pinterest Profits: Quick and Easy Business Growth Hacks

A step by step guide to using Pinterest to grow your website, business, and brand.

Richard Rembert

XSCAPE
PUBLISHING
xscapepublishing.com

Our Company

In 2019, Adrian Kennedy began publishing books for independent authors from his office in Charlotte, North Carolina. His goal was to provide authors with more options and control over the publishing process at prices anyone could afford.

Today, the family owned and operated, Xscape Publishing company still continues to honor the founder's tradition of providing high-quality products and valuable services to the community.

First published by Xscape Publishing 2020

ISBN 978-1-7342856-5-9

First edition

Contents

Introduction

Hey! Thank you for buying a copy of "Pinterest Profits: Quick and Easy Business Growth Hacks." Before I go into the details of how you can make Pinterest work for your brand and business, allow me to quickly introduce myself and share a bit about my unique relationship with Pinterest.

My name is Richard, and I am the content creator behind Rich Point of View Photography, where I encourage and empower photographers and creatives to build their digital empires through blogging & creating digital assets. More specifically, I use my platform to help photographers and online creatives increase their traffic and income with various tips in the photography industry as well as digital marketing.

Back in 2018, struggling as a freelance photographer in New York, I was thrown into a world full of possibilities (too many to test them all!), attempting to get the news out there about my photography and grow my business. That was when I first thought about blogging to bring in awareness and views to my business.

I immersed myself in SEO and digital marketing, but the truth is that I barely scratched the surface! After launching my first website, www.richpointofview.com, my organic traffic continued to grow. What I was doing was working! I've implemented a lot of new strategies since then, but the one that paid off the most was Pinterest.

I started using Pinterest in September 2018. In the graph below, you will see that my blog traffic evolution was closely connected to the development of my Pinterest strategy and efforts.

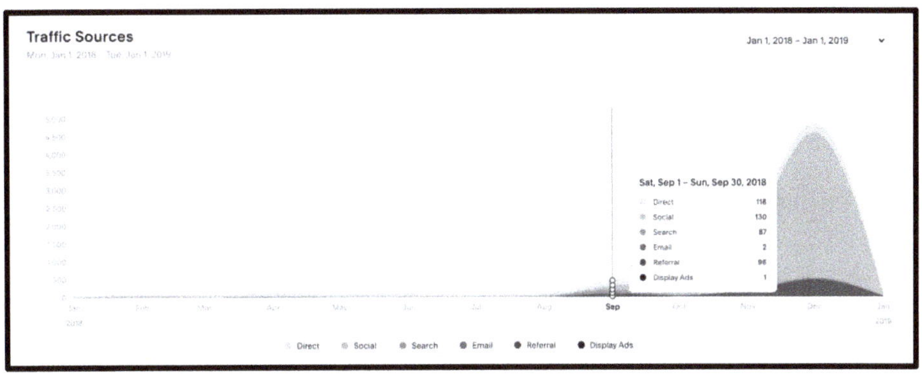

To give you an overview of my Pinterest evolution, here are a few interesting facts and numbers:

- In 2018 (a few short months after I became active on the platform), Pinterest made up nearly 80% of my social traffic through referrals & clicks. (Keep in mind that I was heavily involved in growing other social media platforms at the same time, and none of them came close.) During that year, social traffic made up 78% of my overall traffic.
- In the first three months of 2019, Pinterest already made up 90% of my social traffic. (I've put less effort into other social media platforms, but I haven't increased my Pinterest workload either. Just more evidence that consistency works, and that Pinterest can really take off with a good strategy.)

Source	Visits
Social	6,556 (78.0%)
Pinterest	6,087
Twitter	313
Instagram	128
Facebook	29

UPDATE: 2019 ended with a total count of just under 60,000 sessions generated by Pinterest ALONE!

Source	Visits
Social	56,823 (77.5%)
Pinterest	55,955
Twitter	1,110
Facebook	76
Instagram	61
Pocket	2
LinkedIn	2

- Since I've started my business, Pinterest has made up for over 80% of my overall traffic. Besides the obvious benefits of growing my blog, Pinterest made it possible to monetize my website, grow my email list, make over 5 figures in affiliate sales in my first year of blogging alone, and sell over 5 figures worth of digital products so far.

INTRODUCTION

After various failed attempts at mastering every single social media platform, I decided that focusing on only one platform at a time and mastering it before moving on to the next is the one most important thing I can do for my blog growth.

I'm hoping that you're planning to do the same, now that you have invested in this book. Every second I spent learning about and working on my Pinterest strategy came back ten-fold.

Meanwhile, my Facebook traffic is nearly non-existent since I stopped being active there. My Twitter traffic is coming along with me as I'm, taking it more seriously for my business and showcasing my skills and knowledge. My Instagram efforts go unnoticed because of the ever-changing algorithm and the follow-unfollow game.

I'm not saying to forget about all other platforms. They still bring me traffic, and I know that they can be great marketing tools (depending on your message and audience), but they don't even come close to Pinterest. Imagine: what if you could make Pinterest work for you, even when you can't be there to pin every day? What if you could grow an engaged following, get known in your industry, grow your email list, and make more money blogging through Pinterest?

It's attainable. More than that... I'm here to show you how to make it possible!

As a side-note, I think my Pinterest is doing well, but it is not exceptional compared to other accounts out there. And that's because my audience is restricted to only photographers & creatives, which is a tiny percentage of Pinterest's total users count when you think about it.

If you run a blog that speaks to a broader audience (there are way more moms or health-conscious individuals out there than bloggers, for example), you're fishing in an ocean of potential, and you should expect to see much more significant results coming from Pinterest than me!

About The Book

To put it simply, "Pinterest Profits: Quick and Easy Business Growth Hacks" is a step-by-step guide to optimize traffic and engagement to your website using Pinterest, creating a profile that stands out and crafting a long-term strategy that you can easily automate.

This book is not your standard guide to Pinterest. It goes well beyond how to create a profile and put up lovely board covers. It also taps into the core of how Pinterest really works, and more importantly, how you can make it work for your business to maximize your online presence and make a lot of money without having to spend ad dollars.

So, while this book will pave the way for content creators who are just starting out, for every chapter that's aimed at beginners, I've included a section for business owners.

This will help you strengthen your foundations and double-check that you've done everything right from the start. (Please, don't skip those chapters!) After that, the book goes into detail about more advanced strategies and things I've picked up over time that will help you elevate your current Pinterest strategy to gain more clients and have them buy your digital assets.

There is a lot of information in this book, and I recognize that it might be a bit overwhelming if you're just starting out.

As tempted as you might be to read the entire book in one sitting, I suggest reading one to two chapters at a time and then taking a break to give yourself space to take some action.

Implement the steps, test it out, tweak it, add your own spin on things, really take time to understand what you just did, and only then move on to the next chapter. Your business and blog will thank you for it in the long run.

Take this opportunity to double-check if you're actually **DOING** everything you need to or everything you know you should do, once you come across an "old" strategy or tactic.

And, as a final note on this book, as much as I believe in the strategies I've included in here (because they worked for me and for other businesses and bloggers that I've met), I have to disappoint you and let you know that **THERE IS NO MAGIC FORMULA** to your Pinterest success.

We're continually looking for this magic formula that's going to be universally applicable, but that doesn't exist. If you want this book to make anything possible for you, then take what you learn from it, apply it **ONLY** if you think it will work for your audience and **TEST EVERYTHING!!!**

Reading Instructions

I recommend reading the chapters in the order they are in, with breaks in between to give you a chance to make some real changes to your Pinterest account/strategy.

If you decide to skip to a specific chapter, the information there should still make perfect sense, as long as you know the basics and have set up a business account already.

I suggest reading this on a desktop web browser rather than on a mobile device for better user experience (and this will allow you to check out the resources or tools that I link to through the book as well).

If you think I missed anything or have any questions about the tips, tricks, strategies, and practices, I included in this book, email me at richard@richpointofview.com and let me know!

Now let's leverage your business on Pinterest!

Getting Started With Pinterest

If you're not new to Pinterest, you might be tempted to skip this chapter. May I have your attention for a moment, before you do that?

Besides the detailed aspects of setting up an account and all the technicalities that you might not be interested in, if you've been on Pinterest for a while already, this chapter will also help you understand how Pinterest really works and how it can benefit you as a business owner.

If you don't know that and don't know how your potential readers or clients are using Pinterest, you might miss out on an opportunity to reach them.

Is Pinterest Worth It?

If you're reading this book, chances are that you already believe that Pinterest has untapped potential to get your business in front of more people - your people. You would be right!

Here are some fun facts about Pinterest that will hopefully inspire you to take Pinterest seriously:

- As of March 2020, more than 200 billion pins[1] have been saved on Pinterest. How many of them are yours?

- Last year was pretty amazing for Pinterest. A billion-dollar year, in fact. Checkout this in depth article to see how Pinterest stats measure up against other social media networks[2] and beyond.

- Pinterest became a billion-dollar business last year, earning $1.14 billion in total revenue. The platform's revenue grew 51% between 2018 and 2019, thanks in part to a 46% spike[3] around the end-of-year holidays. Pinterest also attributes its growth to an increase in demand from new advertisers and advances in its conversion optimization products.

[1] https://business.pinterest.com/en
[2] https://blog.hootsuite.com/social-media-statistics-for-social-media-managers/
[3] https://www.wsj.com/articles/pinterests-revenue-topped-1-billion-in-2019-11581037446

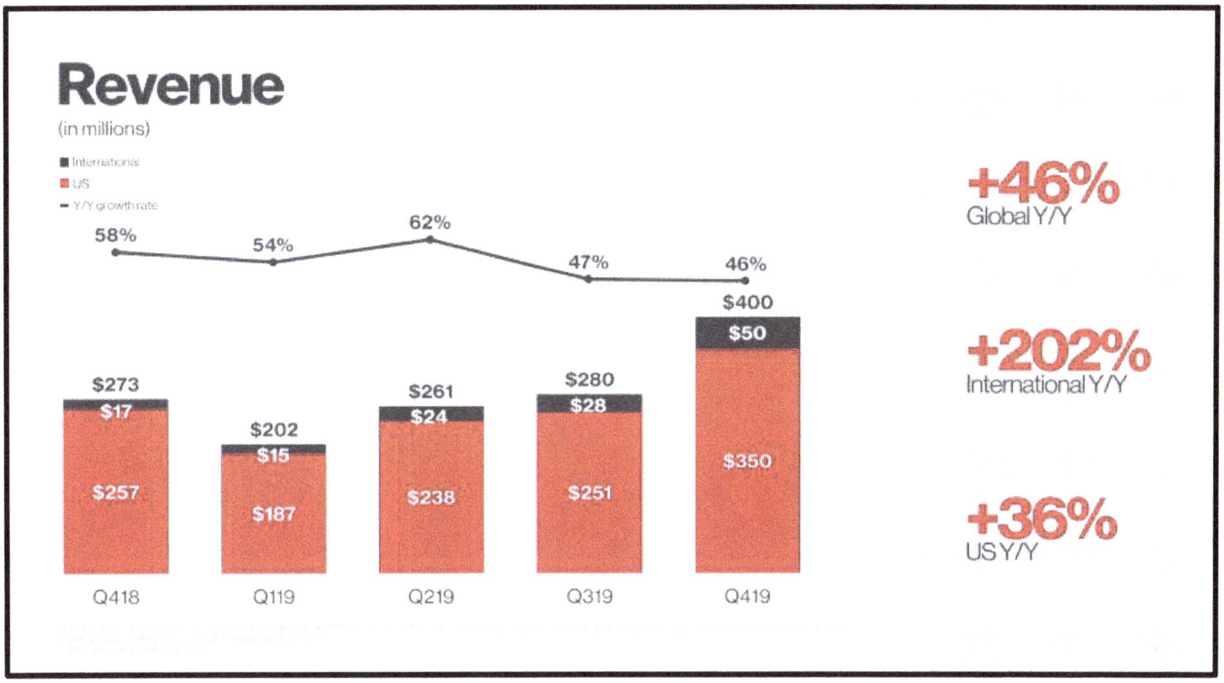

Pinterest is more of a search engine than a social network, and Pinners act accordingly. At 48%, shopping is a top activity for Pinterest users, ranking just after viewing photos (57%). Sharing content, networking, and news all rank as lesser priorities.

This comes in stark contrast with other social media sites. For Facebook, shopping ranks as the 7th most popular activity at 14%. The same goes for Instagram, Snapchat, and Twitter, all of which see lower purchasing rates.

Social Media Activities on Select Social Networks by US Social Media Users, Nov 2018
% of respondents

	Instagram	Facebook	Snapchat	Pinterest	Twitter
Viewing photos	77%	65%	62%	57%	39%
Watching videos	50%	46%	50%	19%	32%
Sharing content with everyone	49%	57%	47%	21%	33%
Sharing content with one to one	33%	45%	49%	13%	20%
Networking	25%	36%	20%	11%	29%
News	19%	38%	15%	9%	54%
Finding/shopping for products	10%	14%	4%	48%	7%
Promoting my business	7%	6%	4%	4%	7%

Note: n=2,500
Source: Cowen and Company, "Facebook: US Ad Buyer Survey and Consumer Survey Highlights; Model Update," Jan 10, 2019

245232 www.eMarketer.com

How Do Your Potential Consumers Use Pinterest?

Whenever I try to teach Pinterest to someone, I ask them to take a couple of hours and just use Pinterest as a consumer. Forget about your own blog or your business, and just go on Pinterest and use it as a simple user looking for something to purchase or read.

If you've never done it before, it will help you understand how Pinterest works as a platform, and you'll have a better understanding of how to use it for your benefit (which is vital to know before you move on to the next few chapters).

- If you're totally new to Pinterest, download the app, create an account and start using it for fun. Get familiar with how it works.
- If you know how Pinterest works, go on it anyway and try to picture yourself as a potential customer. How do they use Pinterest?

If you know how it works already, it will give you a new perspective on how to reach your ideal client/reader because you can start picturing what features they use most and how you can get your content in front of them.

For example, if you run a fitness & health blog and want to build an engaged audience of single mothers, how do you imagine them using Pinterest? Really put yourself in their shoes, or better again, try to ask a friend how they use Pinterest and try to gather insight into how other people spend their time on the platform.

The strategy I teach in this book has to be modified and tweaked to fit your blog/business niche and to reach YOUR target audience, which will differ from business to business.

This small exercise will teach you to pay attention to the aspects and features on Pinterest that will make the most significant difference for you, and you'll be able to have a more substantial impact much quicker.

How Does Pinterest Actually Work?

If you've spent any time on Pinterest this year, you probably already know how Pinterest works.

But do you really understand it?
I like to picture Pinterest as a combination of 3 things (all of which have impacted the way I see the platform and helped me perfect my approach, grow my account and increase my blog traffic):

1. Library of Visual Content

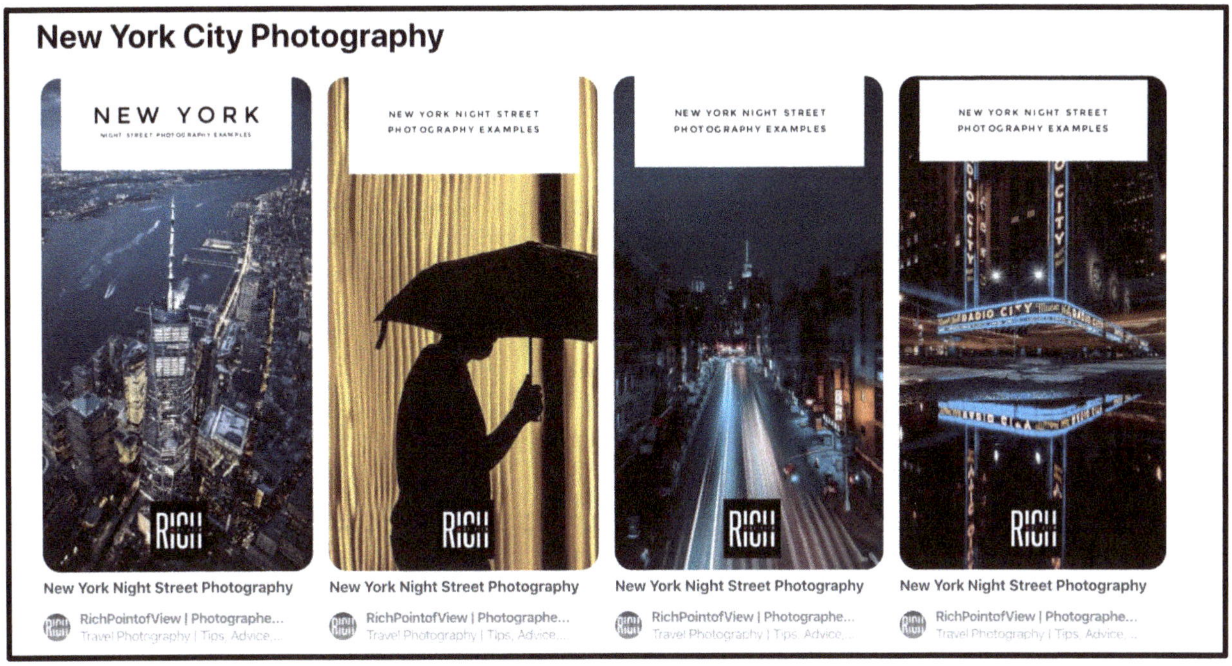

Pinterest is a visual library of content that thrives on getting shared multiple times. Every piece of content you see on Pinterest is called a "pin," it shows up as a picture in a grid or gallery of (usually tall & vertical) images.

Unlike Instagram, where everything is visual, and there's nothing more to it, Pinterest hides a unique piece of content behind every picture. In other words, nearly every pin is linked to a web page where it originated from.

For example, if you click on a picture of my photography print, you'll probably end up at my eCommerce website that sells prints. And if you click on a graphic that promises to teach you "10 Ways To Eat Healthy", you'll be directed to a blog post with this title.

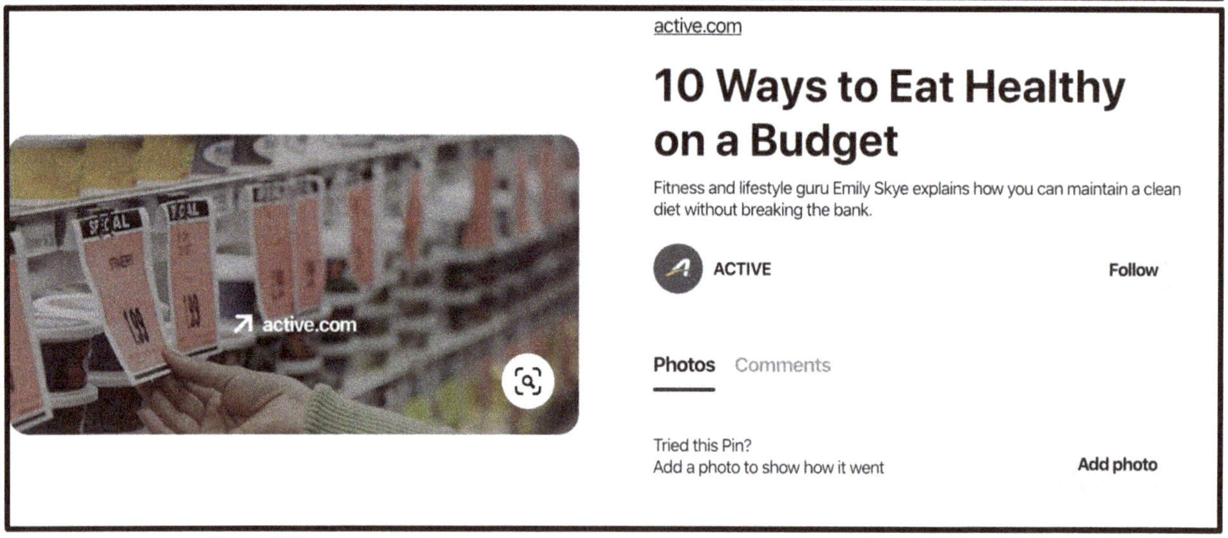

Based on our activity, Pinterest arranges for us to see relevant pins (most of them are from people we follow or pins similar to the ones we interacted with) in the Pinterest homepage, that's called a Smart Feed. This leads us to the second thing that Pinterest is:

2. A Bookmarking Website

Pinterest is a library of curated content on almost every topic imaginable. More than that - it's a visual bookmarking website where we love to store, categorize, and save pieces of content, ideas, and photographs.

Regular consumers use Pinterest to collect all their research, ideas, and findings in the same place. Pinterest is also a visual library that helps consumers sort through the bookmarks they saved quicker (because you can quickly tell what they are by glancing at the pin).

As content creators, we have to know how to capitalize on that. For example, let's say that you're a food blogger, and you post a recipe for a gluten-free brownie and a picture on your website. Someone comes across that post and wants to save the recipe for later, so they pin the brownies' image in their "Healthy Desserts" board.

Unlike Facebook, where people might think twice about what they share with their family & friends, people use Pinterest as a bookmarking vault, and they save EVERYTHING that's of interest.

And we get to benefit from that, because once that picture becomes a pin, we start getting traffic from Pinterest, through no effort of our own.

3. A Search Engine

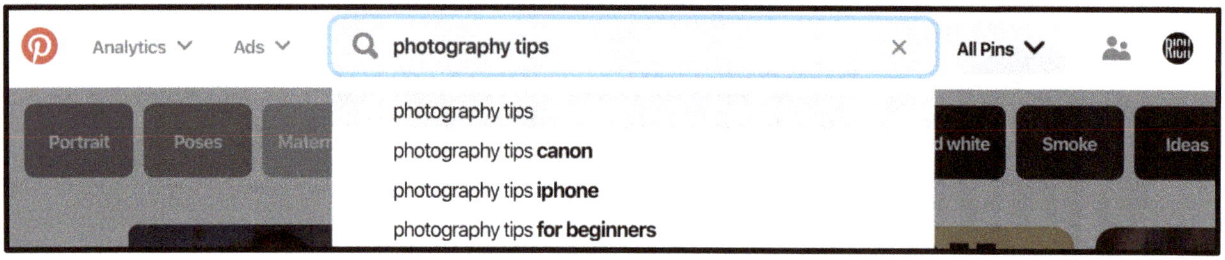

Because of all the above, Pinterest has become a vault of content that is strategically split into categories (known as boards), and is easy to navigate because everything is visual. For consumers, that means that whatever they are looking for, Pinterest has it!

For content creators, that means that you have the upper hand in getting your blog posts, products, or services in front of people that are actively looking for it. Have you noticed how I haven't said that Pinterest is a social media platform - not once? That's because people don't use Pinterest to connect with other people, like other social media platforms.

People utilize Pinterest to discover new ideas and get inspired. Which means Pinterest functions as a search engine (such as Google). And that's good news for us because Pinterest makes it so much easier to get found and noticed by the right people. (I'll show you exactly how to optimize your accounts and pins for this to happen, a bit further along into the book.)

Pinterest thrives on content! Since so many users are using it as a tool to find whatever they are looking for, Pinterest loves fresh content, and they love bloggers and businesses that contribute high-quality articles and images.

Pinterest loves sending traffic to content creators because they know that if their users found what they were looking for on Pinterest once, they will come back for more.

I wanted to show you the benefits of using this platform and give you an insight into how it works first, so you can understand why every step of this book is so crucial to your overall action plan.

Just to wrap things up before I move on to the technical part, here's a recap of how and why Pinterest can benefit you if you're a business owner and content creator:

- **Pinterest thrives on content.** This means they love to champion online creatives and business owners to help them get their content in front of Pinterest users.

- **People share EVERYTHING they find interesting on Pinterest** (by pinning it - which automatically links back to the website they pinned it from), which means that you can get traffic from Pinterest by posting all of your content without having to spend ad money (you can obviously enhance your traffic by doing so if you wish)

- **Pinterest is a search engine.** People use it to search for ideas, information, and inspiration. And who doesn't want to have their content discovered by people who are actually looking for it?

The rest of this book will show you how to effectively take advantage of these 3 facts and use them in your favor. For example, you will learn how to encourage people to save pins from your website to Pinterest and how to get those to show up in search results.

But first, it's absolutely crucial to have a Pinterest presence of your own. If you've been on Pinterest for a while, this is the part you may or may not want to skip. Be sure not to overlook so that you can revise your account and make sure nothing is missing!

A Pinterest Business Account

Create A Business Account

The first thing you'll want to do is to go to www.pinterest.com and create a new business account. After filling out the initial information, Pinterest will walk you through the rest of the very simple and straightforward sign-up process.

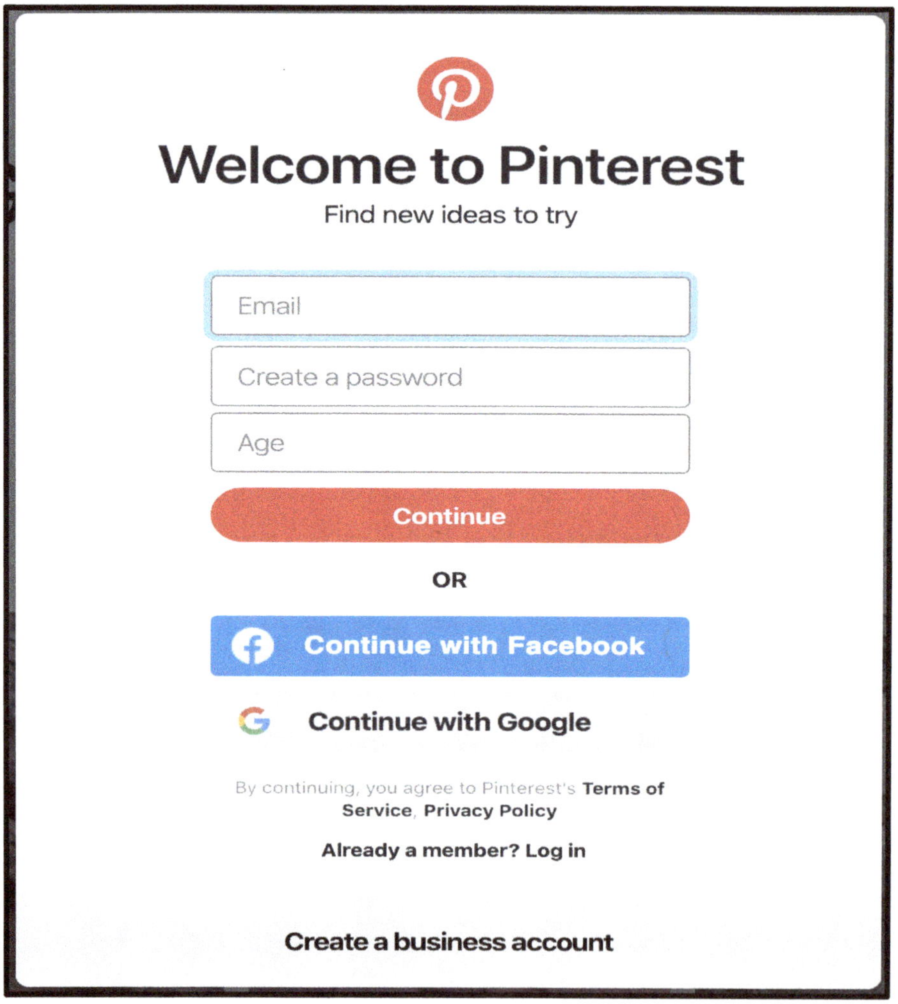

You don't have to be registered as a legal business entity or pay anything to have a business account, it's totally free.

If you're using Pinterest as a content creator rather than a simple consumer, having a business account offers you some useful features such as rich pins (I explain what these are below), better account analytics, and the opportunity to promote your pins.

A PINTEREST BUSINESS ACCOUNT

If you have a personal Pinterest account already, you can switch to a business account by going to http://business.pinterest.com and clicking on the red "Convert Your Existing Account" button (or from your profile settings).

If your personal account is relevant to the topics you blog about, you can simply convert to a business account, clean up some of the irrelevant boards by making them secret, and optimize your performance based on the tips I share further along in this chapter.

If your business or blog is on an entirely different topic, and your current Pinterest account is cluttered with a lot of irrelevant pins, I would start off by creating a brand new account.

Claim Your Website

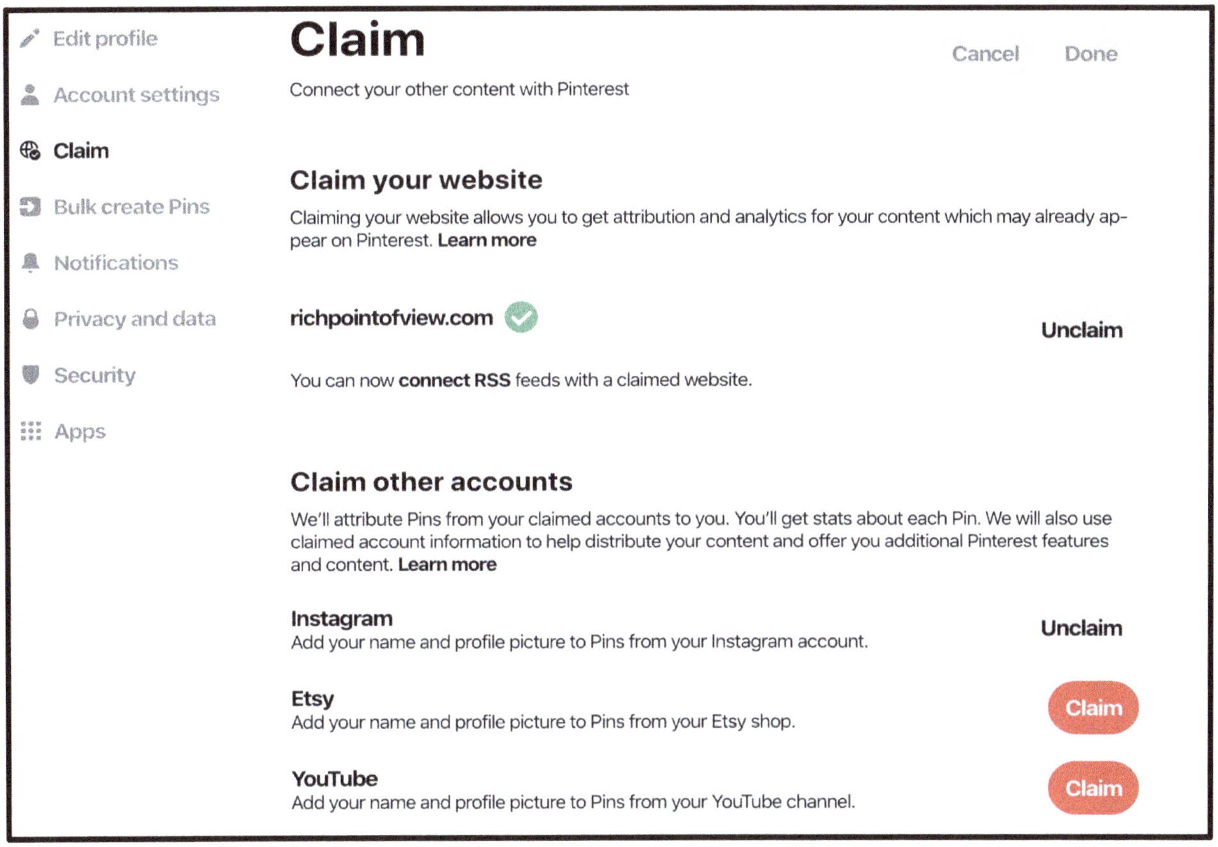

When you fill out your personal information, you will also be given a chance to add your website URL. But to get the full benefits of listing your website there (such as your profile picture/logo saved at the bottom of every pin that comes from your blog and better website analytics), you must first claim your website.

This pretty much means that Pinterest needs to confirm that the website is yours to give you access to more information about how it performs on Pinterest.

As you can see, you can also claim your Instagram, Etsy, and YouTube for organic traffic. Doing so, you can boost your analytics for those sites and products.

Authorize Rich Pins

Rich pins are like regular pins, except Pinterest pulls out some more extra information from your blog posts (such as title, article excerpt, author information, and a call-to-action button. It makes your pin stand out, and it increases your chances of getting clicks.

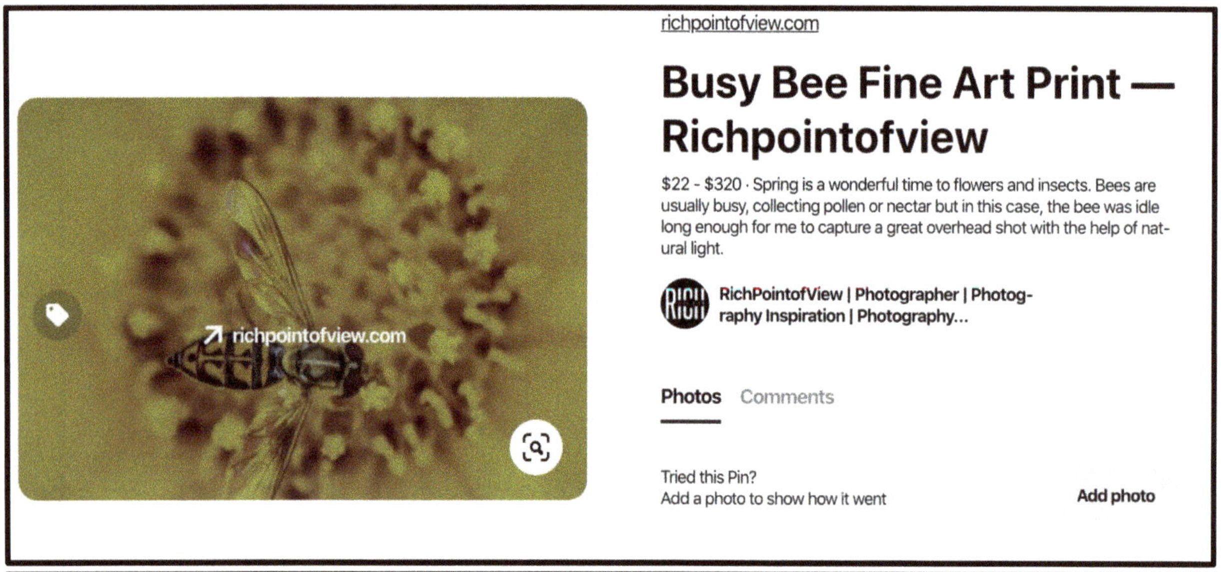

I highly recommend setting up your rich pins from the start (or as soon as possible if you haven't done it already), because it will give your pins an advantage right off the bat (even in the feed). You can see in the examples above.

Pinterest's tutorial on how to enable rich pins[4].

After you've set everything up, don't forget to validate your rich pins[5] to finalize the process.

Establish Your Profile

Now that we've done the hard part, it's time to focus on what our readers, consumers (or other Pinterest users) see when they get to your public profile.

There are specific actions you can do to make your profile stand out, increase your chances of getting found, get more followers, and even drive traffic to your website. I'm going to walk you through each step with examples so you don't get confused.

(If you've already passed this part in your Pinterest journey, take a moment to look at examples below and see if there's anything you can improve on your Pinterest profile.)

Remember, when I told you that Pinterest is a search engine? Search engines usually operate by scanning every bit of content they can find and pick the best results to show whoever is doing the searching.

The excellent news with Pinterest is that you can actually optimize your entire profile to make sure that your account and content are going to be displayed in relevant search results.

For starters, the keywords you use in your name/title affect your entire Pinterest profile. Your board names, descriptions, and pin descriptions play a massive role in your Pinterest SEO.

Pinterest picks up the keywords that you include in your profile to determine which results to show you in. It's important to remember that these keywords have a ranking and that they influence other searches.

---

[4] https://help.pinterest.com/en/business/article/rich-pins

[5] https://developers.pinterest.com/tools/url-debugger/

For example, if someone is searching for a "photography" board, whose board do you think is more likely to pop up? Someone named "RichPointofView Photography" or "James"? Exactly!

The same rule applies to when people search for pins. If those pins are located on boards that have relevant titles and descriptions, you'll rank higher.

In time, Pinterest starts associating specific key phrases and words of their own (even if you don't spell them out on your profile) based on the activity that surrounds your account.

I'll dive into all this more in-depth further along in the book, but what I want you to remember is that the words you choose to display on your profile matter.

Be sure to research your niche and pick your keywords wisely!

Your Name / Title

To edit this, go to Settings[6] > Profile > Business Name

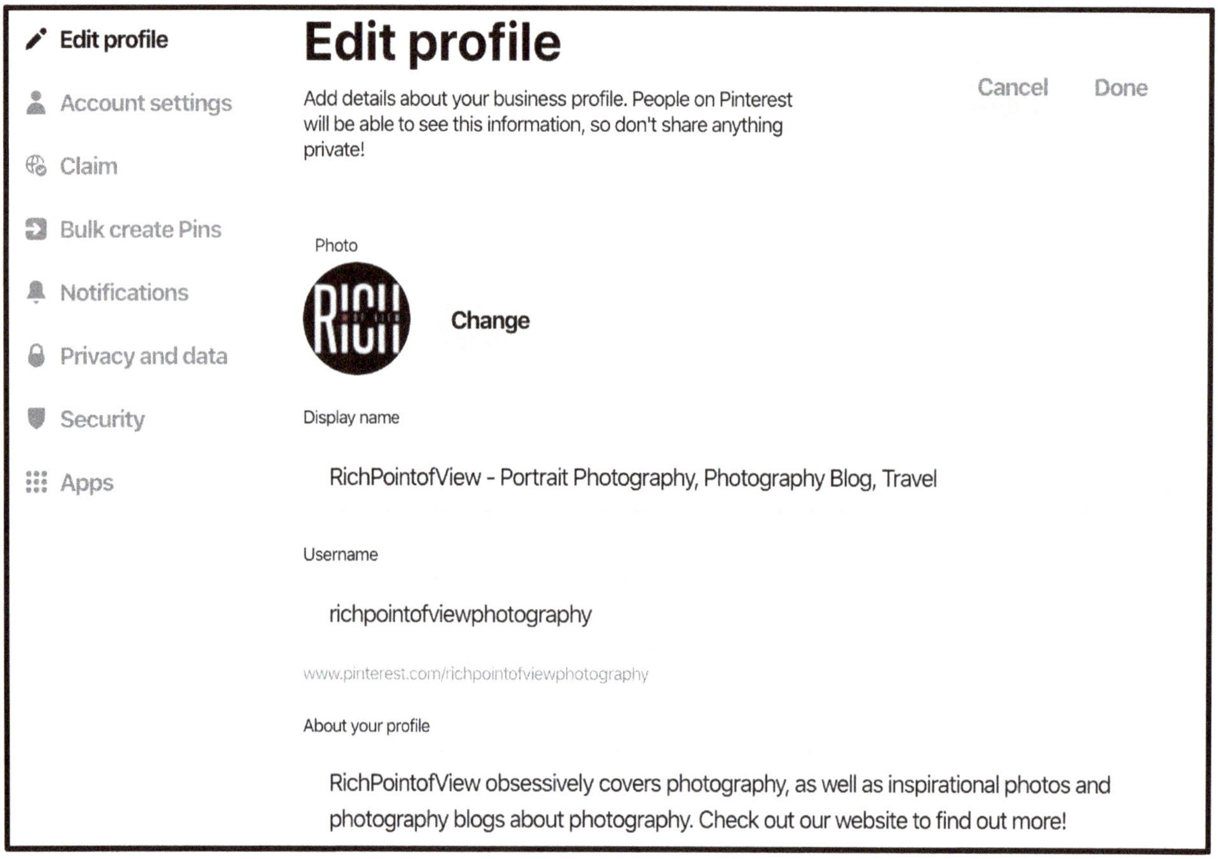

[6] https://www.pinterest.com/settings/

When choosing your Pinterest name or title, people make the mistake of only writing their own name or their blog name. But, in reality, no one ever goes on Pinterest searching for "RichPointofView" or for my full name.

So why waste such precious space on words that bring no value to your overall SEO rank in Pinterest (unless you're already a highly established brand or personality)?

Your Pinterest name should do two things for you:

- Tell people what your profile is all about.
- Get new people to find your account by adding relevant keywords in there.

For example, my Pinterest name gives people a general idea of my profile ("photography blog" - this also helps people find me in the search results), and then covers 2 more specific aspects of my expertise ("portrait photography" + "travel" - two topics I blog about the most).

To find out what the best words to use in your title are, you might need to do some research in your niche, but here are a few other brilliant ideas for Pinterest name that stand out:

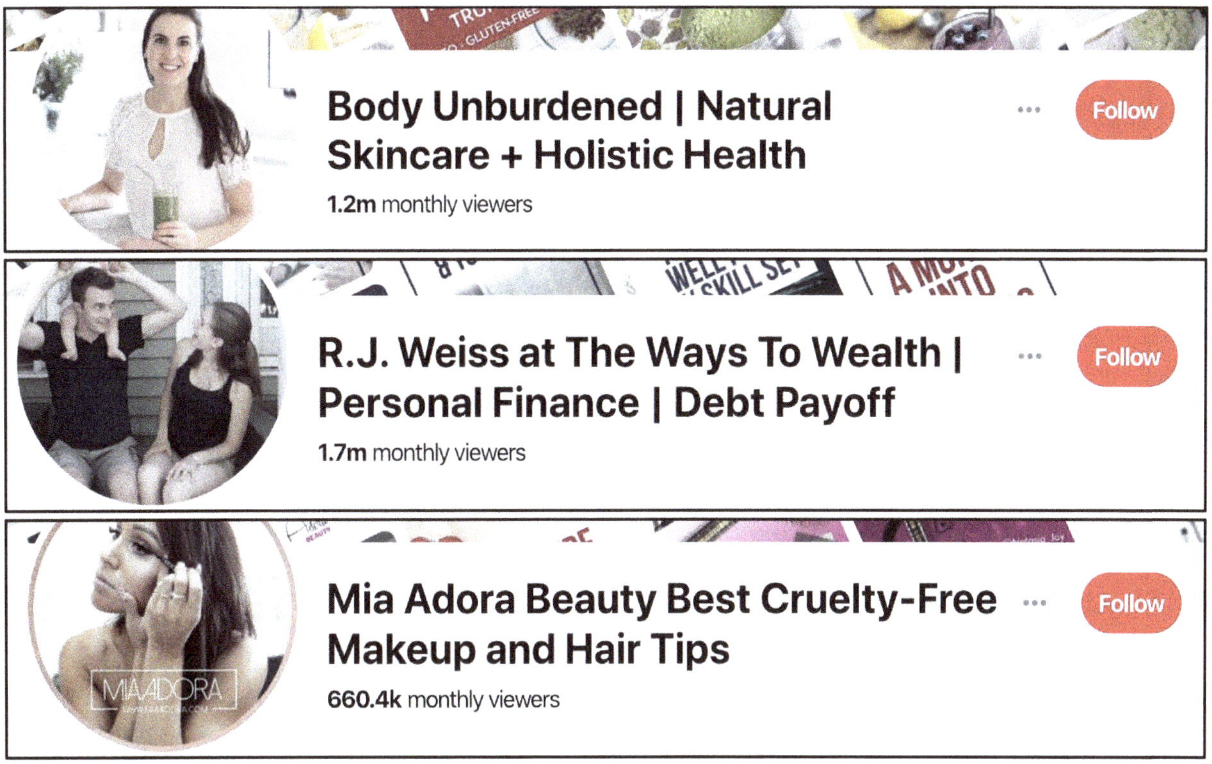

As you can see, they all explain in just a few short words what their Pinterest profile is all about (which increases the chances of getting quality followers), and they often use searchable keywords for their niches such as "natural skincare," "debt payoff," or "makeup and hair tips."

Pinterest only allows 65 characters in the title. If that's not enough to get your key topics out there, download the mobile app, go to your settings, and change your name/title from your phone.

Your Username

To edit this, go to Settings > Profile > Username

Another small tweak that you might want to make to your profile is to adjust your username to make sure it's easy to type, because this will appear at the end of your Pinterest account URL.

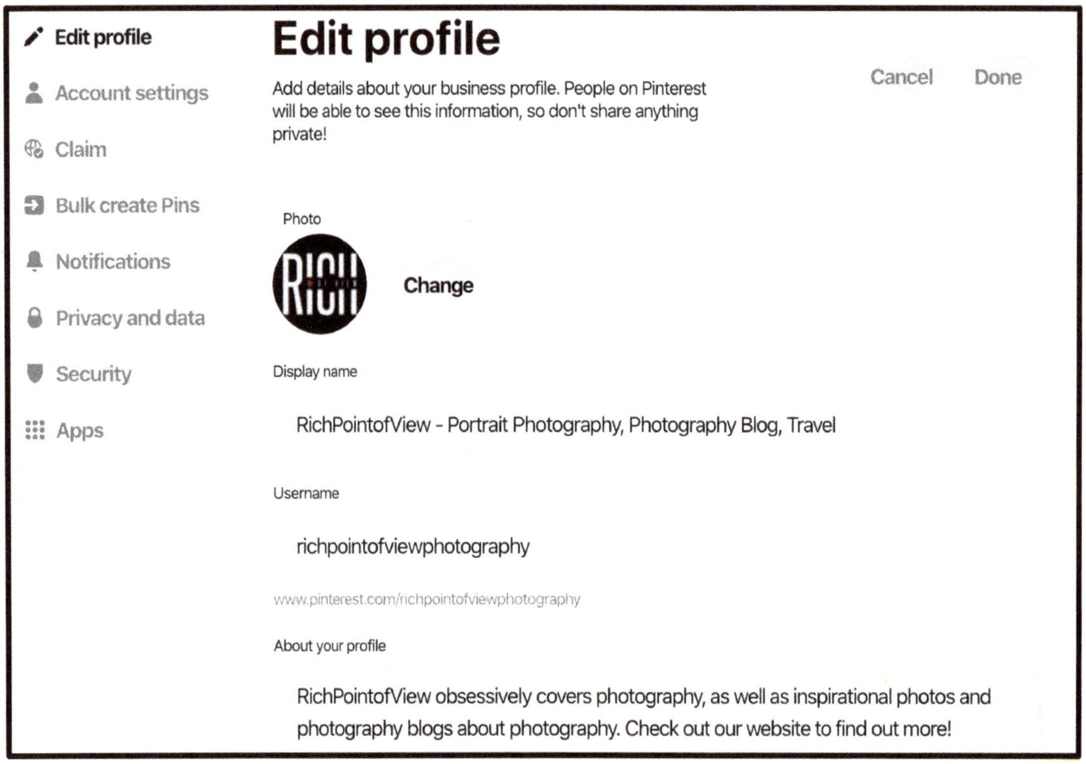

If you were generated a random link such as "xyz145," make sure to switch it to something relevant, like your blog name. As far as I know, this won't count in terms of SEO, but it's essential to be consistent with your social media URLs.

If you change your URL, make sure to go back to your blog and change the link to your Pinterest account as well because otherwise, you will send people to your old account URL, which will be a dead-end page.

Your Profile Picture

To edit this, go to Settings > Profile > Add/Change Picture

Because Pinterest is such a visual place, people sometimes make snap judgments (like if they should click on your profile or follow you or not) based on your profile picture.

This picture is a huge part of your brand, because that's how people recognize you online. So, make sure to use the same picture on all your social media profiles and on your blog as well. Your business/brand will thank you later for this!

About You

To edit this, go to Settings > Profile > About You

Much like your Pinterest name, your "About You" section has the combined role of telling other users about how you can help them and telling Pinterest what your account is all about.

This limited space of characters is your chance to get people to take an interest in what you do and make sure that Pinterest puts you in front of the right people/consumers (remember - they take into account every word you use in your profile).

In other words, this is where you want to be very selective about the words you use because they matter. This is also an extra opportunity to rank for keywords that didn't fit into the title.

And here are a few more people that understood the importance of their profile bios:

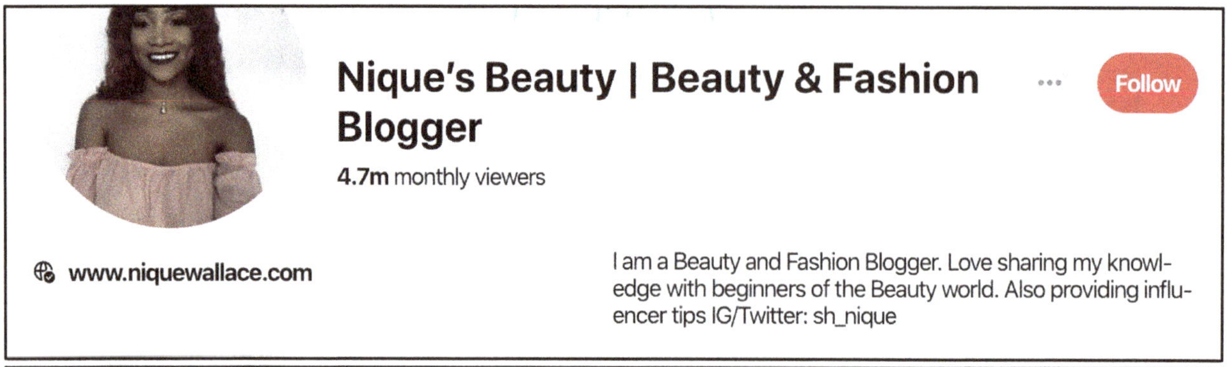

Not only have these people used their bios to promote IG pages or existing freebies, but they took advantage of their bios to insert keywords such as "beauty and fashion blogger," "tech training" and "meal prep recipes" that will really help their accounts get noticed in those niches (by both people and Pinterest's SEO).

Organizing Your Pinterest Boards

Once you have your profile all set up, it's time to move on to the other crucial aspect of your account: your boards.

Pinterest boards serve as albums of content that help users efficiently categorize all their pins, to make them easier to find (for both themselves and for their followers).

Types of Boards

There are three types of Pinterest boards: public boards, secret boards, and group boards. In this chapter, we're going to discuss the first two, leaving group boards a section of their own because if you are reading this book, you have joined the Facebook Group with various group boards in it already. (Yes, they are that important!)

Public Boards

Public boards are your own personal boards that can be seen by your followers on your profile. When you pin something in there, that pin usually shows up in the feed of your followers (but not always, since the Pinterest feed is not entirely chronological).

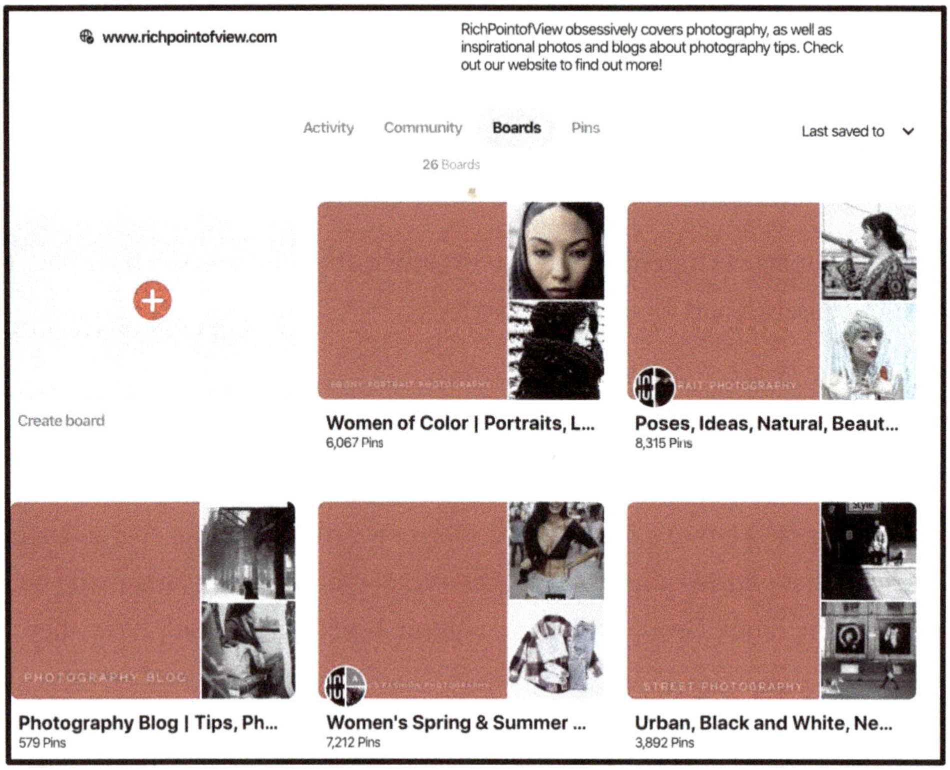

These boards are created, owned, and managed by you, which is why they are also called "personal boards." Your followers can see them, but they cannot alter them in any way or pin anything. You get to decide everything that goes into that board, including the title, description, and board cover.

Personal boards are the foundation of your Pinterest profile, and choosing them wisely plays a big part in forming a solid Pinterest strategy.

Ideally, when creating a new Pinterest account, you will want to start off by having at least 5 personal boards relevant to your niche and to your followers. If you've been on Pinterest for a while, you can start adding up to these, aiming to have at least 10-15 personal boards on your profile.

These boards need to be inter-connected and make sense as a whole. They also need to speak to your target audience more than they speak to you.

It's very tempting to create boards for everything we have in mind, and everything we're interested in, and I think that's a mistake that most Pinterest users make in the beginning, myself included.

The reality is that having boards on every topic under the sun is only going to confuse your potential followers.

Take a few minutes to brainstorm board ideas by including what your business is about, the topics you may blog about, what you want to be known for on Pinterest and what other relevant boards might be of interest to your audience.

For example, I created "Photography Blog" and "Social Media Marketing" boards, because that's what I blog about. I also want to be known for "Portrait Photography" and "Travel Photography," so I added separate boards for those sub-topics.

I also included boards such as "Home Office" (because my audience is made up of bloggers and online entrepreneurs that do a lot of work from home and "Home Décor" is a popular Pinterest topic), "Food Styling," and more relevant boards, that make sense as a whole because they address the needs of my audience and still fit my overall profile theme (even if I personally don't blog about or photograph them often).

Before going forward, brainstorm a few ideas for boards in your niche and start off with 10-15 boards of your own. You can always go back and add more as you get more ideas or expand your business or change your blogging topics even further.

Make sure to include every single category and subcategory that your business offers, what you blog about, but also other topics that you know your readers might be searching for on Pinterest. Look at similar accounts to yours and see what type of boards they have included and aim to break big topics into multiple boards. (For example, I have a Travel Photography board, but I also created a subcategory inside the board with various locations that I've been and cover in blog posts, because Pinterest loves specific, niched down boards, and so do people!)

If you're not new, go back and review all your existing boards and make sure they speak to your audience. Have a good look at your profile and make sure that they all fit together based on the things you've learned in this chapter!

For example, if you're a fashion brand, avoid creating boards about recipes and parenting. Instead, try making some boards about fashion trends, frugal shopping, DIY clothing, and so on. If you're a home decor stylist, avoid creating boards about fashion and create boards for each room of the house, advice for homeowners, vintage furniture, and so on.

Please note that, for example, if you consider yourself a parenting AND finance blogger, it's excellent to make that known in the profile name and then include boards that are relevant to both categories.

Or, if you're a fitness brand, you have the liberty to choose multiple subcategories for your business/blog, and therefore you can cover various topics on Pinterest as well.

I'm not advising you to make your profile about one thing only unless that is your area of expertise/niche, and that's the only thing you want to be known for.

From my Pinterest research, I discovered that more specific, niched down accounts seem to be more popular, because people know exactly what they are going to get when they follow them.

If your Pinterest account is about 10 different things, and someone is only interested in 2 or 3 of those topics, they might not be inclined to follow you because they don't want their feed full of pins that are not of any interest to them.

But when you clarify what your Pinterest account is all about, and you create boards that cover different aspects of the same topic or point of interest, not only are you going to get more followers, but these followers will be 10 times more engaged with your content because every pin you post will be of interest to them.

Your Main Board

Out of your personal/public boards, the most critical board that you can create is your mainboard.

Your mainboard will be the board where you only pin content from your own website and add all the Pinterest graphics you created.

Having all my pins in one board also helps me remain organized and gives me a place to turn to when I want to see how my pins perform, schedule them, or edit them. (If you scatter your pins in other boards, they will eventually be buried under other pins, making it impossible for you to find them.) You are also able to pin your pins in other boards you created, but starting off, it helps to keep one mainboard for all original content before you start adding them to relevant boards.

If you don't have any pins of your own yet, you can hold off creating this board just yet, but this should not be missing from your Pinterest account once you start pinning your own content.

This board should always come first on your profile, because it will allow people to look even deeper into your online presence, as soon as they land on your Pinterest profile.

Usually, the mainboard is called something like "Best of BLOG NAME" or "Posts from BLOG NAME," but I also like to include a few keywords after that, to make the board searchable on Pinterest. (Because, once again, people don't really search your blog name on Pinterest.)

If you blog about multiple topics that are not directly related, consider creating numerous mainboards such as: "BEST OF + YOUR BLOG NAME + TOPIC 1", "BEST OF + YOUR BLOG NAME + TOPIC 2" and so on.

Separating topics such as home decor and weight loss, for example, is ideal because, in time, Pinterest learns how to associate a board with specific keywords. (More on this later.)

By creating multiple boards for your business or main blog topics, you help Pinterest understand what your boards are about, and you will help your pins perform better individually.

Secret Boards

These are personal boards that are not visible to your followers. Hence the term "secret."

These boards usually come in handy when you want to save pins for personal reasons (because they would not be relevant to your audience), and they can help you keep a tidy profile, especially if you like to pin a lot of off-topic content for personal use.

Secret boards have no SEO value, which means that they don't negatively or positively impact your account. Create as many as you'd like.

Group Boards

Group boards are public boards that have multiple contributors. That means that multiple people can pin to the same board, and this board will appear on all their profiles.

Every group board has 1 admin - the user who created it - and this person can invite other contributors. To be able to pin on that board, you must first be invited and accept the invitation.

The admin can also decide if she/he wants to let the other contributors invite people or be the only person who can (which is the case with most group boards because people wish to control who joins their boards).

You can recognize a group board right away on someone's profile, because a little circle will appear, featuring some of the contributors.

Group boards are not going to help you gain followers per se (when somebody follows a group board, they only follow that board and not all the contributors), but they are accommodating in growing your reach. (When you pin something to a group board, it's going to be seen by the followers of that board, even if it's not seen by your own followers.)

We're going to go over in more detail about group boards in the next chapter, including how to create them, how to find the best ones for your account, and how to get invited in them.

How To Build A Board

Now that you've made a list of relevant boards, it's time to create them. To do so, all you have to do is go to Pinterest > Your Profile > Boards > Add New.

To create a board or make an existing board secret, all you have to do is edit the board, once you create it, by clicking on the little pencil that appears in the right corner when you hover over a board and click on the "Secret" lock to activate it.

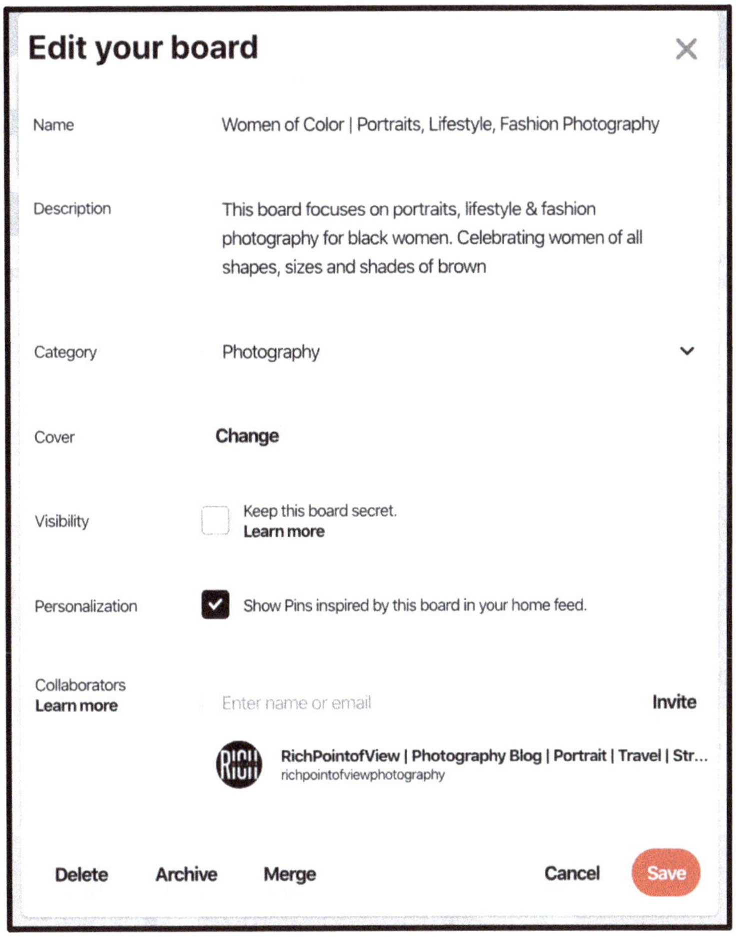

To transform one of your personal boards into a group board, all you have to do is click edit (or the little plus on top, next to your profile picture when visiting a specific board), and use the "Collaborators" function to invite people (via email or via their profile name).

Arranging Your Boards

When it comes to the order of your boards, the type of board will usually indicate the ranking in which it should be placed.

The order matters, because people usually pay close attention to the first 8-12 boards that you have on your profile.

The new default Pinterest profile shows a carousel of 5 boards of your choice, and then it displays your most recent pins. People have to go to your "Boards" tab to see all your boards.

So, you need to be strategic in arranging your boards. This will differ a lot from account to account, based on your business niche and the topics that you blog about most often. I've developed a ranking structure that will help you arrange your boards efficiently:

- The first board on your profile should ALWAYS be your main-board.
- Following this up, you will want to place your personal boards in the order of importance (what you blog about the most, what you want to be known for and after that, topics you might not necessarily blog about often, but that would still be of interest to your audience).
- Afterward, you will want to place your own group boards, if you have any.
- Last on your profile you'll want to place all the group boards that you're a part of.

Remember that whenever you create a new board, Pinterest automatically adds it to the front or bottom of your boards, so you will have to go in and allocate it a new spot, in conformity with this "Pinterest seating chart".

To move your Pinterest boards around, you will have to go to your Profile > Boards and make sure that the "Sort Boards" function is selected as "Drag & Drop." Otherwise, Pinterest will decide the order based on activity or name.

ORGANIZING YOUR PINTEREST BOARDS

Setting Your Boards Up For Success

When creating your boards, there are a few key aspects that you want to take into consideration to make sure you're setting your account up for success. These are the board name, the board description, the board content (the pins that go in it), and the board cover.

Board Names

When naming your boards, avoid being funny, and don't use words that people won't understand or won't be searching for. Keep it relevant and straightforward.

Remember that your words weigh a lot on Pinterest because it operates as a search engine. When people look for boards to follow, you want yours to pop up in the results.

Board Descriptions

After creating the board, don't forget to go back and add a description for it. This is a step that many people overlook because they imagine that no one ever reads board descriptions. This is probably true, but adding a description to our boards is not for our followers, it's for the benefit of getting discovered on Pinterest.

Remember how I said that Pinterest scans our profiles to figure out what they're all about? The titles and the descriptions of your boards play a huge part in that.

When determining how to name and describe your boards, think about what your audience is most likely to search on Pinterest, do some keyword research of your own, and pick your words wisely.

While in the title, you usually get to select one main keyword, the description is the place where you elaborate on that.

If your board is titled "Quick Workout Routines," in your board description, you might also want to add terms such as "easy workout methods," "quick calorie-burning exercises," "5-minute killer ab workout" and so on.

Try adding these keywords in sentences, so that your board description has a flow and avoid stuffing all the keywords that you can think of in there without context.

You want to create descriptions that are formed of real sentences and add these keywords in there wisely. (For example: "Want to start a fitness blog, and you need some blogging tips for beginners? Follow this board to keep up to date with the latest blogging advice and training!")

See how easy it was? And I also included a call to action that humans will respond to, so if they do end up on that board, you have a higher chance of converting them into followers.

Keep in mind that your board titles and descriptions are highly crucial to Pinterest, and they attach that data to every pin that goes into that board. (That's why, if you pin a recipe pin into a recipe board first, it tends to do much better than if you pin a pin to a "random blog posts" board. That data embeds itself into the pin, giving Pinterest more context about it.)

Board Covers

The next aspect of your profile that not many people concern themselves with is the board's appearance - more specifically, the board covers.

Your profile appearance and your boards (so everything we've discussed so far), have a significant impact on that first impression you make on potential followers.

If you really want to grow your account and remain truthful to your brand and memorable at the same time, I suggest taking some time when starting out to focus on your board covers. (I've reached 15k followers on Pinterest, so I know this matters more than people give it credit for!)

Before I dive into that, I just want to say that investing too much time into your board covers and obsessing over them is not recommended. In comparison to other aspects of your Pinterest strategy, board covers fall behind when it comes to the significance attached to them, and that's because the engagement you will receive will be for individual pins in the smart feed/discovery / related pins categories and not on your actual profile.

I think it's worth figuring out a theme for your profile and then spending a little time setting it up when you're getting started, but, as I said, don't obsess over it. (Your time is better spent on optimizing your pins, especially if you're struggling to increase your reach and business traffic, rather than your followers.)

Pinterest allows you to select one of the existing pins in a board as a cover image, therefore, instead of displaying the latest 4-5 pins, they show your chosen picture, with just 2 of the most recent pins to the side.

To give you an example of how this looks, here is a comparison between 2 random Pinterest accounts: one that selected board covers for all their boards, and one that didn't:

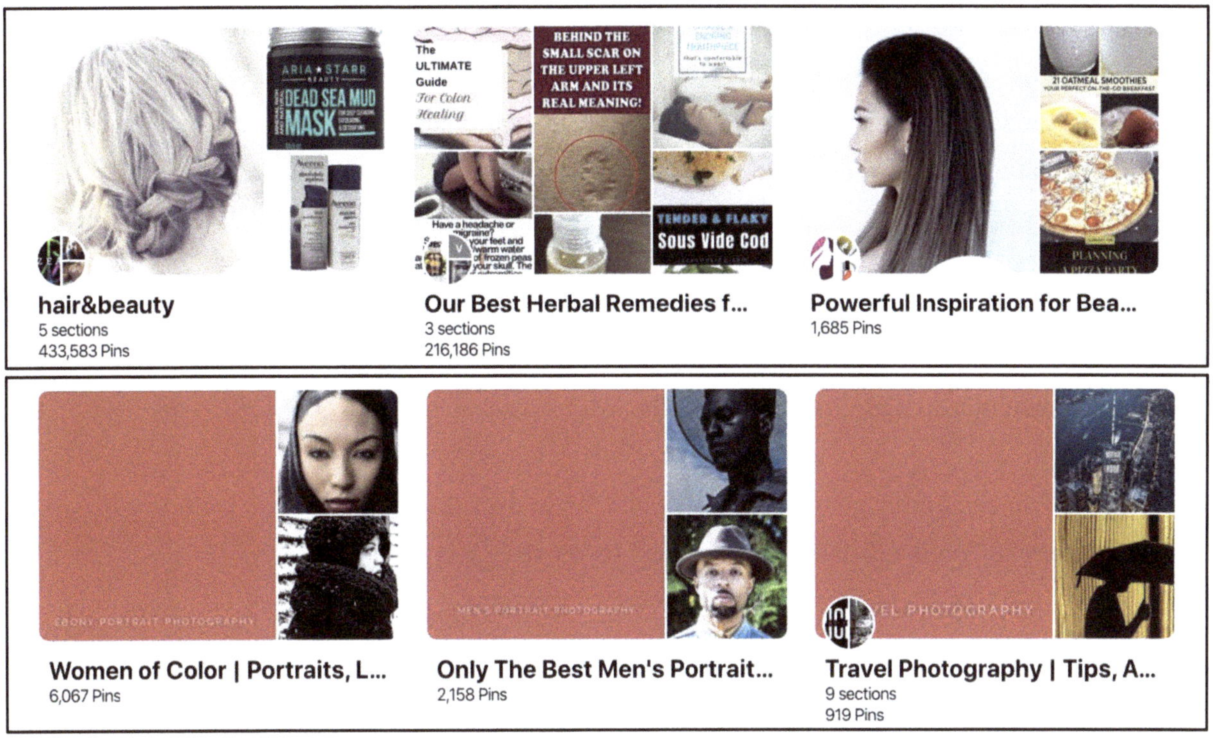

As you can see, the profile without the board cover looks messy, and because the images are so small, it's hard to tell what the board is about just by looking at it.

My profile with board covers, however, looks much more organized, clean, and intentional. You can tell by quickly scrolling through the boards (and without even reading the board titles) what that profile is all about, and in a world where everyone is constantly busy, you want your potential consumers to be able to do the same.

I believe that selecting board covers for your boards can drastically change the appearance of your profile, and this is a feature you can use to make sure your branding comes across as intended.

We're going to talk about how to brand your pin graphics soon, but your branding needs to start with your boards. For example, I went with a custom-made board cover for my Main board, where I displayed my logo because I wanted people to instantly recognize me as they land on my profile.

My brand colors and dynamics are carried throughout the rest of my board covers (they are all red, and I've often used my own pins as cover images, deepening the connection to my brand and website) even if they are not custom made, or designed using a template.

There is no one way to do this right. Selecting a board cover in the first place is a must! Think about your Pinterest profile like an Instagram grid. You have to make sure that your pictures belong together when scrolling, even if you choose not to create board cover templates like the examples above.

Most importantly, be sure to stay true to your brand aesthetic and brand colors. (In other words, if your logo or website colors feature a lot of yellow and green, have board covers in either yellow, green, or both.)

How To Create and Select Board Covers

If you've decided to create your own board covers, you will have to create square 1x1 images (800x800 pixels is what I use) and then upload them to that specific board.

Once you do that, you can simply go to your profile and hover over the board that you want to edit. Click on the pencil icon, and click on the "Change" button next to "Cover".

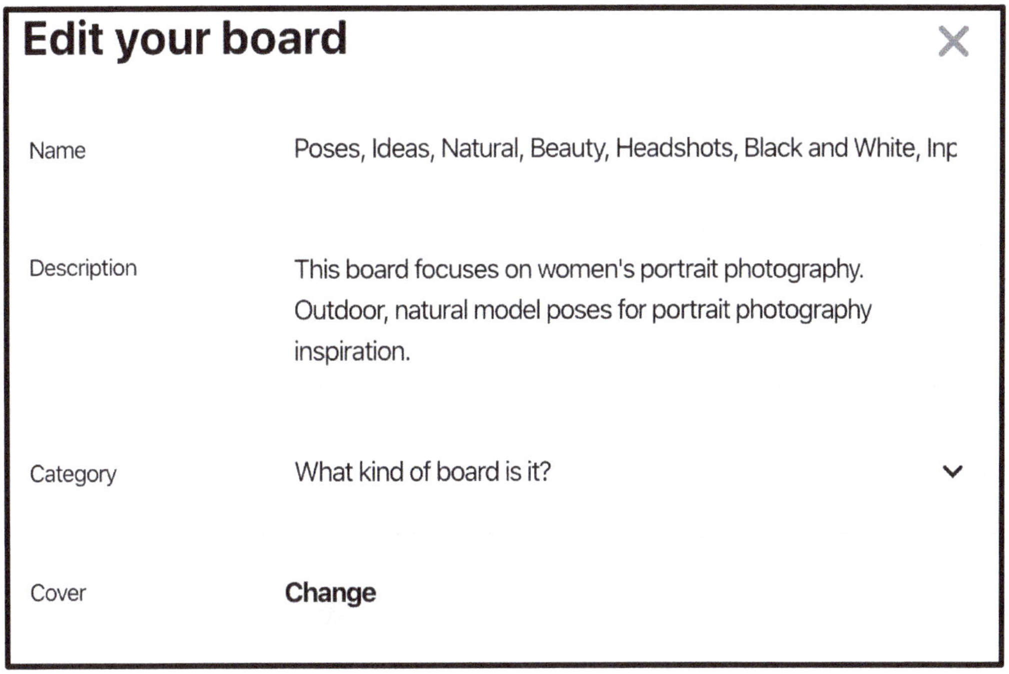

Pinterest will then pull out the pictures in that board and select the one you want, all you have to do is move the arrow to the left or the right, position the pin to fit the square that shows up, and save the change.

One of the main reasons I always place my group boards last on my profile (no matter how relevant or significant those group boards are, to begin with) is because you cannot change their board cover, and they end up looking messy and unorganized on my overall profile.

Luckily, people don't usually scroll that far along on your Pinterest profile, so your first 5-10 boards need to look pristine, and that's where board covers can make or break your account.

Even if they mess up your profile's appearance, group boards are a vital part of expanding your Pinterest reach. In the next chapter, we're going to be focusing our attention on how to get the most from group boards - once you find and join them! But first, a quick note about board sections.

Board Sections

I've seen a lot of people who have more board sections than they have boards. Big mistake! Sections are a new feature that is only meant to help with user experience (if people land on your board - which rarely happens anyway).

Sections do not help with SEO. Therefore, if you create a board and add a lot of random sections, this will only confuse Pinterest's engines.

So be sure to create separate boards if you've gone too crazy with your sections, and only use them when the topics in hand are very similar (or when you have an off-topic board that you want to organize).

You can also use sections for your mainboard to give people an overview of the topics you blog about and allow them to browse through all your posts easily (but as mentioned earlier, if your subjects are not closely related, I would create multiple main boards instead).

Maximizing Your Group Boards

As we've already discussed in the previous chapter, group boards are public boards that allow multiple pinners to contribute and share their pins in the same place.

Pinterest group boards are instrumental tools that allow you to circulate your pins, gain traction, and get them in front of people who don't follow you on Pinterest.

Recognizing A Group Board

You can recognize a group board by the fact that multiple profile pictures of the contributors are shown in the corner, either when you look at it amongst other boards, or when you visit an individual board.

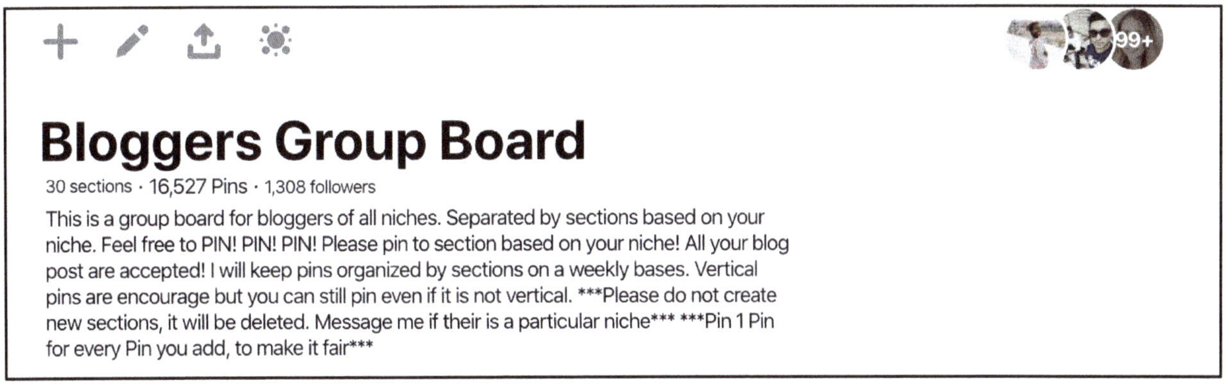

Functional group boards also tend to specify their status in the description (if they are accepting contributors or not), and ideally, they should contain some sort of instructions on how you can apply to join.

Benefits of Joining Group Boards

Group boards have one admin - the person who created that board - and the significant majority of followers that the respective group boards have belongs to this person.

Joining group boards is one of the simplest ways to boost your Pinterest reach (even with a new account). Here's why group boards can increase your reach, help you grow your account, and get more traffic to your business/blog:

Gain More Followers

Once you become a contributor to a group board, that board starts showing up in your profile. If a group board has 100+ contributors, that board is now showing up on 100+ Pinterest profiles, which means it has a way bigger chance of getting discovered and followed by people.

When somebody follows you, they only automatically follow your own boards. Group boards have to be followed manually, which is why, most of the time, the followers of a board belong to the person who created it.

When joining group boards, a rule of thumb is to pick the ones who have more followers than you. Back when my account had less than 2k followers, I got into group boards that were followed by 5k, 10k, and even nearly 500k people, and this is why group boards can explode your reach!

Even when you join boards with the same number of followers as you, you are still doubling your reach. (Whenever you pin something to that board, it shows up to an entirely new demographic. Hint: extra eyes, clicks, and repins for your pins.)

Better Activity

Since they have multiple contributors, group boards tend to be more active than our regular boards (even if we try to pin regularly).

Pinterest loves activity! Therefore, they tend to reward group boards, and show pins added there often in the smart feed of users.

Reciprocity Rule

Most group boards have a reciprocity rule. Since they know that Pinterest loves active boards with good engagement as well (aka boards that are getting a lot of repins), board owners tend to request collaborators to repin pins from that group board.

This will look like "for each pin added, repin a pin from this board" or "repin at least 10 pins per month from this board." It varies from board to board.

This creates a platform of mutual sharing, where you don't only benefit from the added exposure of adding your pins there but are also seeing good engagement from other contributors.

Group boards allow you to drastically expand your Pinterest reach and share your pins in places with a high level of activity where they stand a better chance of getting noticed. It's a win-win situation for your business.

Finding Group Boards to Join

So now that you're convinced that missing out on joining group boards would be a big Pinterest mistake for your brand/business, you're probably wondering where you can find some to join.

Before I share with you my favorite ways to go about looking for group boards, here are a few things you should know when picking which ones you want to apply to:

- **You want to apply to boards that have at least as many followers as you have,** but ideally more. (Once your account is big enough - over 5-10k or so - you might want to join smaller boards than you as well because they tend to be more engaged and they still benefit your account.)
- **You want to join at least 20-30 group boards.** That's just in the beginning. But what I'm trying to say is that you can never join too many, so think big.
- **You want to join as many niched down, super-specific group boards as possible.** These are the boards where your pins are going to perform the best! There are a lot of boards out there that are universal and that allow you to promote whatever pins you like, and if they have a big following, those can be helpful too, but the most important thing you need to do is to join as many boards that are relevant to your niche as you can.
- **You want to join as many boards owned by people in your niche.** Because the majority of people who follow a board belong to who created it, the boards of people who have similar accounts to yours are going to be much more valuable than boards owned by random accounts.
- **You want to join group boards that have under 200 collaborators.** While active boards are great, crowded ones don't seem to do as great. The sweet spot for most boards tends to be between 20 and 100 collaborators.

Speaking of people in your niche, that's a great place to go looking for potential group boards to join. Below I will list a few ideas of places where you can find active group boards to join.

Look For People in Your Niche

A great way to start is by looking up people on Pinterest that have a similar account to yours (they blog about the same topic, they are experts in your field, or they are simply other Pinterest users that you found via searching that pin about the samc topics) and scour through their group boards to find relevant ones that you might want to join.

You already know how to recognize group boards, all you have to do is scroll down when looking at their boards (make sure you select the "Boards" overview when you land on their profile) and open in a new tab all group boards that seem relevant.

Don't only stalk people in your niche, befriend them as well. A good tip for being a part of exclusive boards is making friends with content creators with similar content and starting a group board together. This will be a goldmine for all of you since your audiences will be similar, so your pins will see great engagement.

Pin Groupie (Yes, it's a real name)

There is a website called pingroupie.com[7] that was built to deal with this Pinterest dilemma. Pin Groupie is essentially a directory of Pinterest group boards that allows you to quickly search boards by their title or description and find relevant boards in your field.

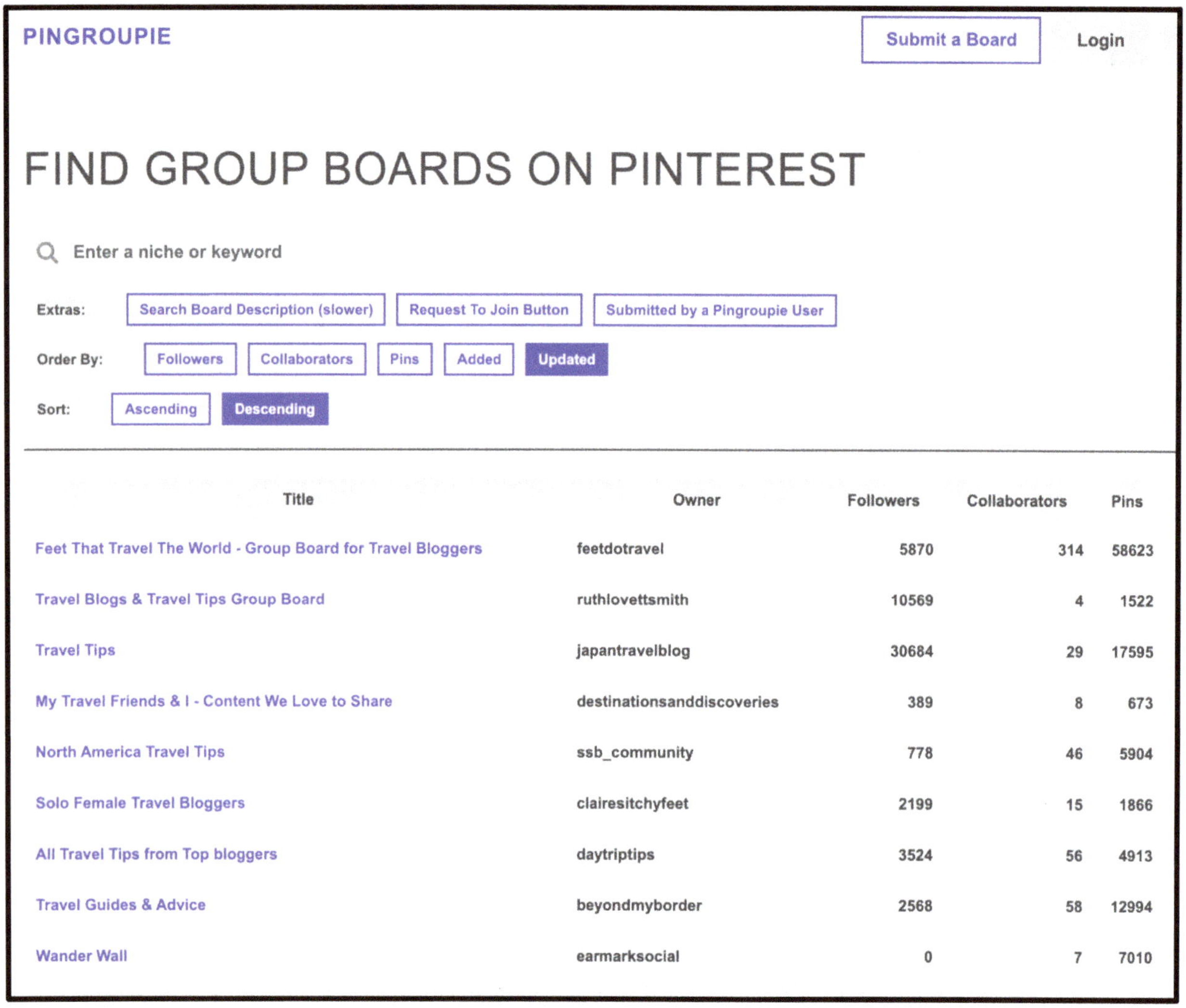

PINGROUPIE

Submit a Board Login

FIND GROUP BOARDS ON PINTEREST

Enter a niche or keyword

Extras: Search Board Description (slower) Request To Join Button Submitted by a Pingroupie User

Order By: Followers Collaborators Pins Added Updated

Sort: Ascending Descending

Title	Owner	Followers	Collaborators	Pins
Feet That Travel The World - Group Board for Travel Bloggers	feetdotravel	5870	314	58623
Travel Blogs & Travel Tips Group Board	ruthlovettsmith	10569	4	1522
Travel Tips	japantravelblog	30684	29	17595
My Travel Friends & I - Content We Love to Share	destinationsanddiscoveries	389	8	673
North America Travel Tips	ssb_community	778	46	5904
Solo Female Travel Bloggers	clairesitchyfeet	2199	15	1866
All Travel Tips from Top bloggers	daytriptips	3524	56	4913
Travel Guides & Advice	beyondmyborder	2568	58	12994
Wander Wall	earmarksocial	0	7	7010

For boards to be listed here, they require at least 5 collaborators, 50 pins, and 250 followers, which is a great place to start anyway when looking to join boards.

Just make sure you preview the board's description to see if they include details on how you can join. Otherwise, skip it.

[7] https://pingroupie.com/

Always search for an opportunity. I've found Pinterest boards when I wasn't even looking. If you don't have time to apply, save the links somewhere and spend an hour every month sending your applications for all the boards you've hoarded over time.

Joining And Managing Group Boards

Now that you've found and picked the best group boards for your Pinterest profile, it's time to start applying. Each group board will have a different requirement or a set of instructions for how to apply.

Most board owners request that you email them, message them on Pinterest, or comment on one of their most recent pins.

The most important thing to remember before doing so is to click on the first image that appears in the corner (that is always the owner of the board), go to their profile and follow them. You need to follow their entire account (not just the board you want to join), for them to be able to invite you to any of their boards in the first place.

People don't tend to check their Pinterest messages that often, if that happens to be a requirement to join a board, you should try to find an email address of the board owner (by going to their website), and sending them an email too, just to increase your chances.

Accepting Board Invitations

Once you've been invited to group boards, you'll receive both an email with the invitation (that you have to accept by clicking on a button) and a Pinterest notification in your messages/inbox.

In Pinterest, this sometimes shows up under "Contact requests," as shown in the picture below, so always make sure to check that to see if you've been invited to any group boards.

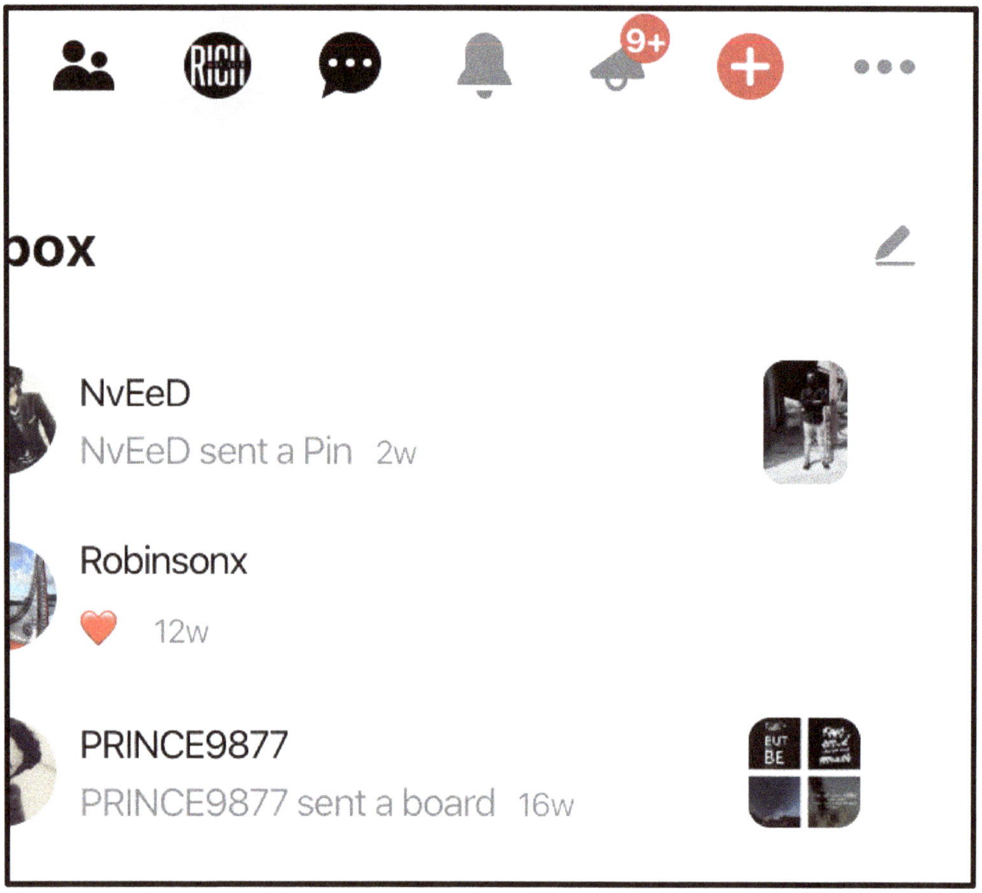

For the process to be complete, you must accept the invitation via at least one of those means.

Once you do, you will become an instant collaborator, and the option to pin to that board will appear every time you use the pin feature.

You will be able to distinguish between your own boards, your group boards, and your secret boards by looking at the icon that they have next to them in the drop-down list that appears when you pin something. (If they don't have an icon, they are your public boards. Secret boards are marked with a lock, and the other icon stands for group boards.)

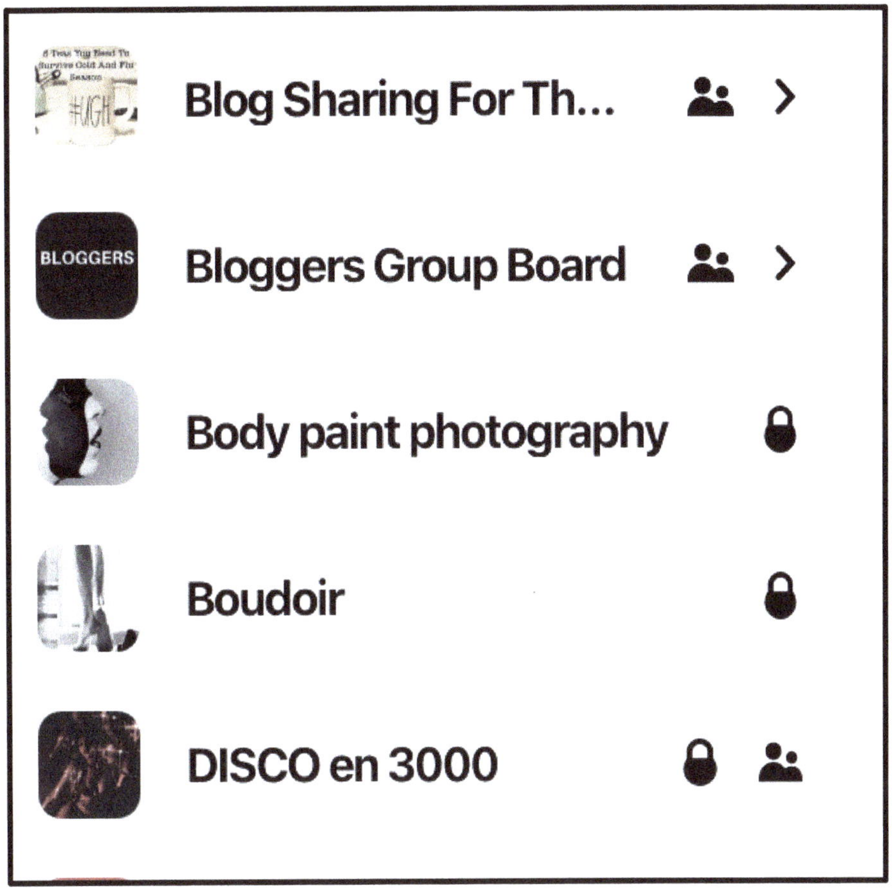

Managing Group Boards

It's vital to keep track of each group board's regulations if you want to remain a contributor to that board. Most boards aren't very closely monitored, but I have kicked and been kicked out of group boards myself for breaking the rules.

When joining group boards, make sure to create a spreadsheet to keep track of things like:

- What you are allowed to pin in that board (some boards will only enable you to pin about particular topics) and what you're not allowed to pin (some boards do not allow you to pin the same image twice, for example)
- If you have to repin other people's pins out of that group board (their reciprocity rule if they have one).

The last one is more important than you know. Not just because you want to respect the rules of the boards you're a part of, but because being engaged with the boards you are in actually helps those boards do better - and therefore, your pins will do too.

Developing Pinterest Graphics

There are two ways you can use Pinterest: a simple consumer/user or a content creator. As a business owner, if you're not using Pinterest as a content creator, and if you're not contributing unique content to the platform, you waste your time.

As I've already mentioned, Pinterest thrives on content, and business owners and bloggers are the heart of their operation. That means they are giving you all the opportunities you need to succeed.

This book is meant to help business owners, bloggers, and online creatives prepare their Pinterest account and form a Pinterest strategy that will help them promote their **own content!** If you don't have any content on the platform, simply having a Pinterest account will not help your blog or business in any way.

The way that you get traffic from Pinterest is by creating pins that link to your content (so, to your individual blog posts, services, and products, for example) and getting Pinterest users to click on those pins to visit your website.

Ideally, you want at least 2-3 images (these are also known as pin graphics) that link back to each and every blog post, sales page, landing page, or anything else that you have, and you want to promote. So again, 2-3 Pinterest graphics for each blog post you write. If you have 10 blog posts, you should have at least 20-30 pins that you created on your Pinterest profile, excluding the actual photos spread throughout your blog.

Some of these images can be just that, images. In specific niches, the photos speak for themselves, and people will click on them because they already know what's on the other side.

Take, for example, recipes, outfit photos, home decor, or make-up images. Even without some sort of text overlay that describes the picture, pins like that tend to do quite well on Pinterest (because Pinterest is a visual platform after all).

In these cases, you won't need to do much, other than pin the images that were already included in said posts (as long as they are tall & vertical) to Pinterest.

In case you haven't used Pinterest before, you pin your content the same way you pin anything else to Pinterest.

The first thing you need to do is install the Pinterest Save Button extension[8] for your website. It allows you to select and save any image to Pinterest by clicking on the Pinterest logo that will appear now every time you hover an image.

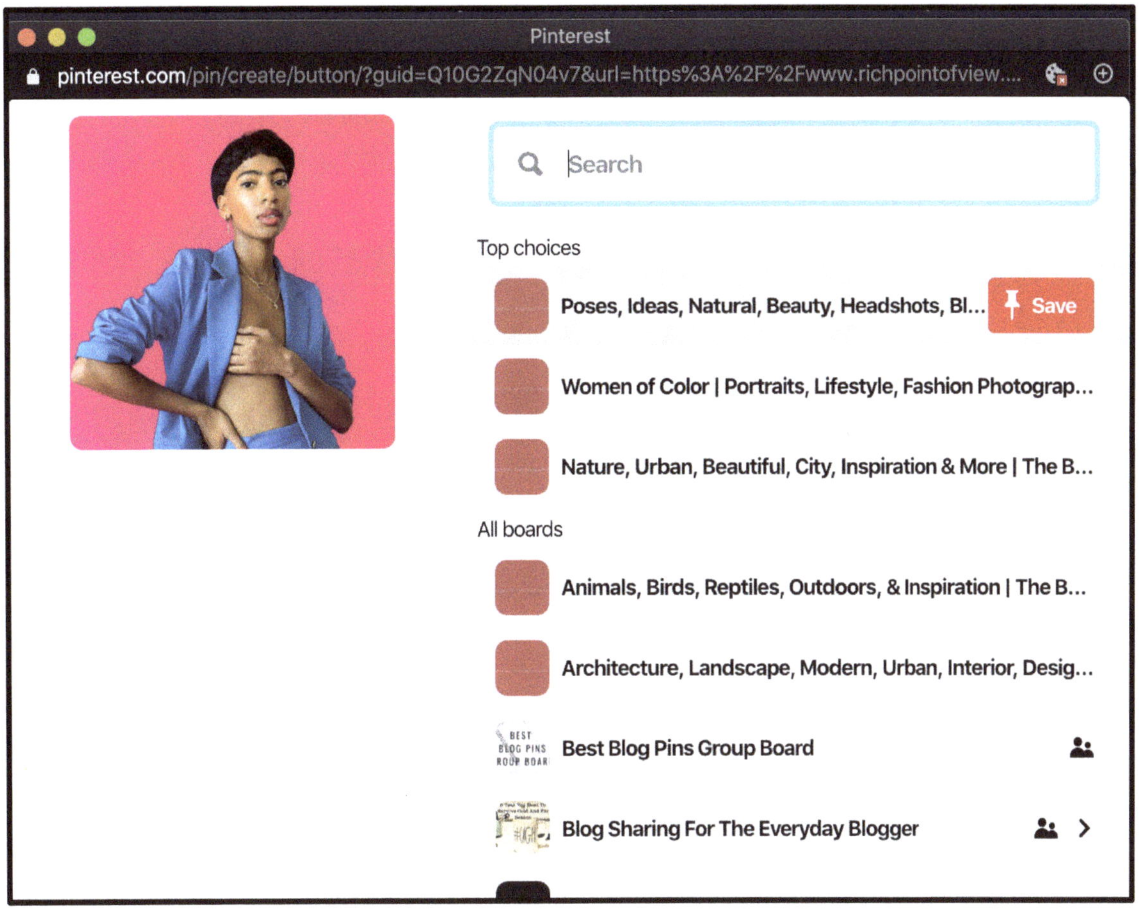

[8] https://chrome.google.com/webstore/detail/pinterest-save-button/gpdjojdkbbmdfjfahjcgigfpmkopogic?hl=en

If you are on Squarespace, you can just go to Marketing > Pinterest Save Buttons and do it this way as well.

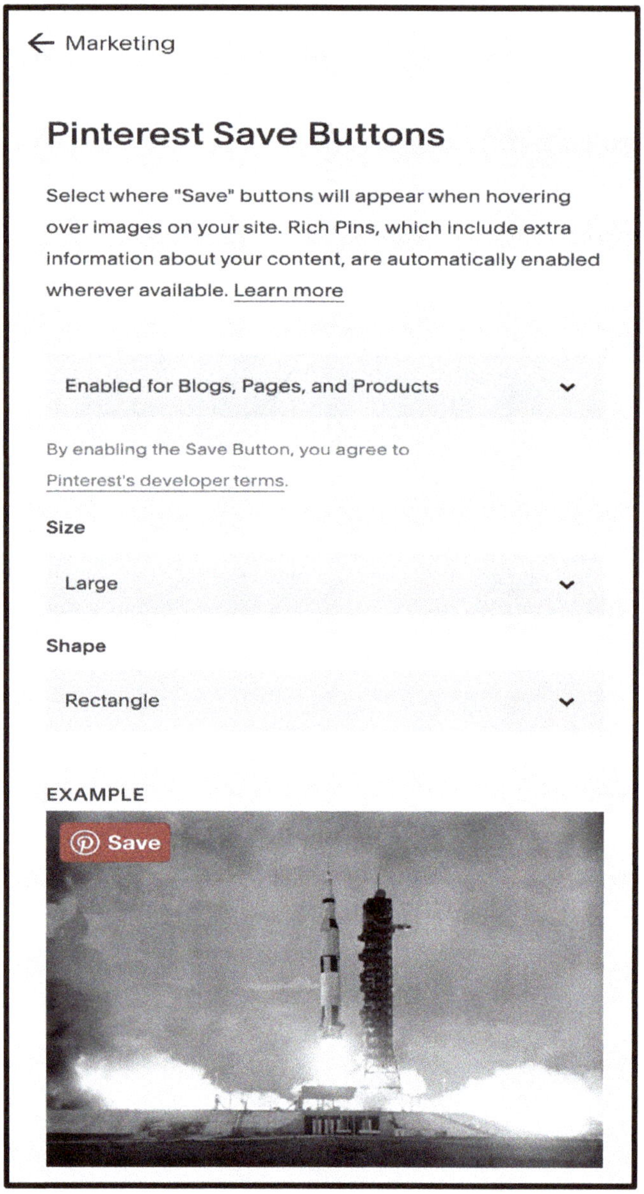

When you click on the icon, a new window will open up, and you will be able to select which board you want the pin to go to, and you can even add a description to that pin. (I'm going to discuss best practices for this in the next chapter.)

The pin will automatically be linked to the URL where you saved it from, or you can go back and edit it to change the destination URL any time after you posted it.

To better illustrate what I'm trying to say (in terms of visual content vs. content that needs a written explanation), I want to offer myself as an example, a photographer.

This blog post is composed of galleries of photos featuring a specific aesthetic for street photography and a short description of what inspired the choices.

I mostly use visual content on Pinterest that will rarely need any additional text overlay for other Pinterest users to understand where the pin is going to lead to.

All I have to do is go to each blog post and pin the vertical pictures on Pinterest (usually to the main board first, then to others as time goes on).

This is just a matter of what catches people's eyes, and that's why it never hurts to have multiple pins/images leading to the same blog post.

The point that I'm trying to make here is that for some niches, the visual content and the photos you create will often make great stand-alone pins, and they are an excellent way for you to start promoting your blog on Pinterest, without needing to do any extra work.

In some other niches, images just won't really say anything to the users, so text overlay is required.

I made sure to create at least four Pinterest graphics, where I explained what the post was about by adding a text overlay. That helped my pins stand out and it encouraged more clicks than the other simple street photography pins.

So, whether your content is visual or not, text overlay (where you include the title of the blog post, for example, in the pin) is always recommended because it encourages clicks from people who are genuinely interested in finding out more. That's the secret sauce of building an audience with the help of Pinterest.

Of course, if your blog topic cannot be covered solely by images, you will have to heavily rely on creating your own Pinterest graphics.

For some niches, even if you could add visual content because everything is open to interpretation, I recommend adding text to your pins. Take, for example, a photo of food - are you teaching people the recipe, talking about your diet and nutrition, or merely showing them how to take stunning food photographs?

If you're struggling to create pinnable content for your blog, this chapter will show you exactly how to create your own Pinterest-worthy graphics, even if you've never done anything like this before.

Crafting Your Own Pinterest Graphic Templates

The heart of getting traffic from Pinterest is by creating pins or graphics that lead people back to your blog posts or website.

No matter what you blog about, at one point or another, you're going to need to create (or get your hands on) your own Pinterest graphic templates.

Allow me to explain. If you have to create a pin graphic (with text overlay and everything) for every blog post you have, you're going to have to start from scratch every time.

That's going to amount to a lot of work and a bunch of graphics that have no resemblance. But there is a way to avoid this: by creating a few Pinterest graphic templates.

Have you ever noticed how most bloggers who have a well-established Pinterest presence, seem to have the same appearance for all of their pins, except that the wording on the pins change to fit whatever blog post they are trying to promote (and sometimes the background image or the structure of the pin differs a little bit as well)?

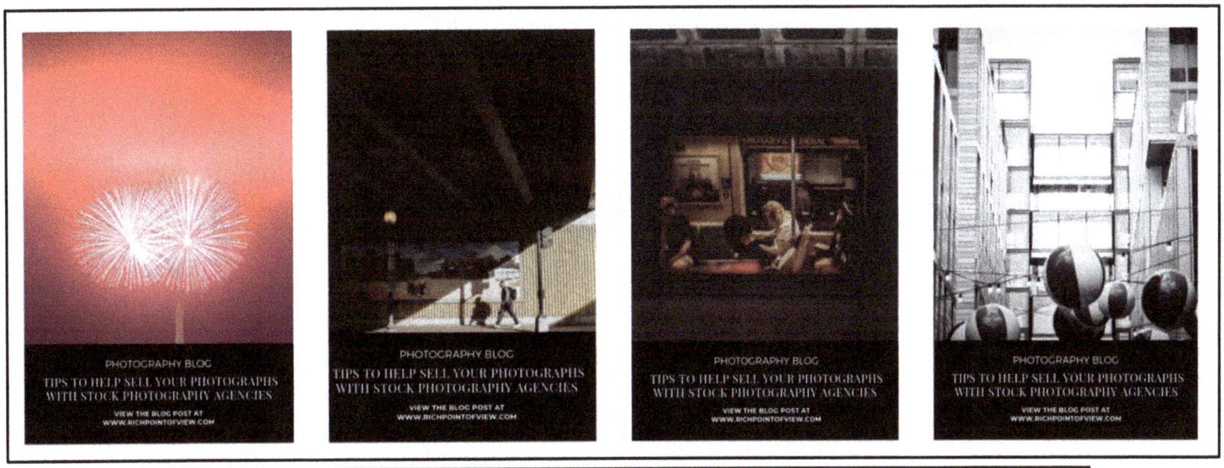

Having templates of your own is such a time-saver when it comes to creating content to put on Pinterest, and, at the same time, it will help you be consistent with your branding and have a well-established aesthetic. (That means you won't have to decide new colors, fonts, and elements for each pin you create because everything's already selected).

Keep in mind that when I mean templates, I mean plural. You should have at least 2 or 3 graphics for each blog post, so you will need to start off with at least 2-3 templates. Ideally, you will want to end up with 4-5 different graphics, but you can start with 2-3 and work your way up.

I recommend you do that because you never know what's going to be more popular. Having 2 or 3 options gives you a chance to A/B test your pin graphics, texts, and pin descriptions, and therefore you'll be able to play around with slightly different versions and see what works better.

This also improves your chances of getting found on Pinterest because, mathematically, 3 are better than 1. So, if you start your blog with 5 posts and only have 5 pins, it's going to take a while before you see any real traffic from Pinterest. But if you create 3 graphics for each post, you'll have 15 pins that lead to your website circulating on Pinterest and, just like that, your odds triple.

So, if you're starting on Pinterest now, start with 2-3 pin templates. If you've been on Pinterest for a while, and have a good collection of pins already posted, create at least one new template and add some new pins for older posts.

There are 2 main ways in which you can get your hands on some pin graphic templates, I will only go into detail about one of those.

Pre-Made Templates

If you don't have a lot of time or patience to learn how to make your own, the easiest and quickest way to get your hands on some graphics is to hire someone to make them for you or to buy pre-made templates.

There are plenty of people who sell their services on Twitter. You just have to do a little digging.

Design Your Own Templates

You don't have to spend money or hire someone else to make your templates. When I started my blog, I didn't have money to invest in something like this, so I decided to learn how to do it myself.

With all the tools and tutorials out there, you can too! In fact, because I knew that programs such as InDesign or Illustrator would have taken me too much time to master (but they are great alternatives if you're looking for ideas), I started creating my Pinterest templates in WordSwag, then moved to Canva[9], and I still do to this very day.

Canva is a free (pay for more options) online design tool that I use to create all my social media graphics, and they actually provide content creators with free templates of their own (called Canva Layouts) that you can use or tweak as you want.

Canva is also super easy to learn, and it can produce some really high-quality graphics if you know what you're doing.

[9] https://www.canva.com/

When I first started with Canva, my pins were ok but definitely not the best. Like anything in life, the more you practice, the better you will get at it.

I don't consider myself a graphic designer now either, but Canva allowed me to improve my skills and to start creating better and better templates on my own.

If you're just starting out, be patient, keep striving to improve your pins, and don't worry too much about the fact that they are not pitch-perfect. In fact, let's have a look at the essential elements that every Pinterest-worthy graphic should have.

Features of A Good Pinterest Graphic

Whether you have decided to buy your Pinterest templates or to create them yourself, there are a few things you need to keep in mind when looking at the design of a pin.

Some of these suggestions are just that - suggestions. They are mostly based on my own experience, hours of research, and just noticing what type of pins tend to do better on Pinterest.

You can conduct an experiment of your own for pins in your niche. Use the Explore Page on Pinterest to look at the trending pins in different categories. See what pops up in your feed most often and what kind of pins you are more likely to notice, read, click on, and so forth. Take notes of what you like and dislike about those pins and apply all that new-found knowledge to the design of your templates.

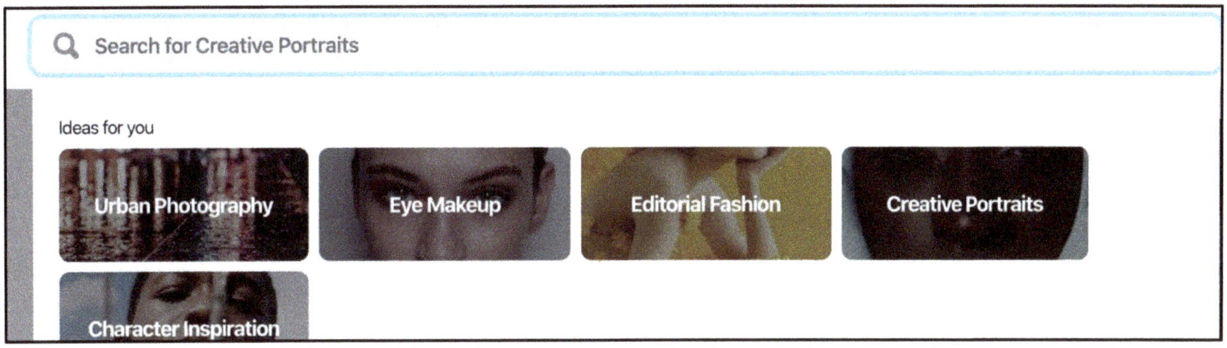

Other elements below are common-sense rules that you need to follow if you want to give your pins a great chance and be taken at face value.

Remember that when you're creating your own pins, you want them to reflect your online personality and your branding - which is, and should be, unique.

Pin Dimensions

Something that I can't stress enough is that your pins should be vertical. That is because pins are organized into columns, so vertical Pins take up more space in the feed and tend to stand out more.

The ideal ratio for a pin is now 2:3, so 600px wide x 900px high or pins that respect that ratio. For example, I found a sweet spot for my pins at 800 x 1200 pixels. (And as you can see, this respects the 2:3 ratio.)

While you definitely don't want to make the pin too short, you don't want to exaggerate it either. If you want your pins to perform well, make sure they don't exceed 1260px in length and conform to the 2:3 ratio.

Pinterest has also declared that square pins might even begin to perform well, but for pins with a copy (text), I would stick with taller images because this allows you to make the text bigger, which means it can be easily read (especially on mobile).

Branding

Branding is an essential concept that your pins should reflect during the creation process. If you're debating on whether your logo should appear on your pins or not, that's not even up for debate as it absolutely should. Elements such as the colors you use, the fonts you choose to go with, and sometimes even your copy, are all components of your brand.

Assuming you use the same pin templates, people will begin to recognize your brand instantly, and they will become more familiar with your content as a result.

You want your pins to draw attention to your content, and you want your branding to be just a subtle (but easy to recognize) aspect of your pins and not the other way around.

Your pins should always include the name or link to your blog, usually somewhere at the bottom of the pin. This helps you increase your brand awareness by getting your name (or the name of your business/blog) out there, and it clearly states that you created that graphic, making it easier to prove to Pinterest who really owns the pin if it ever gets stolen.

If you want to incorporate your logo within your pins, I recommend placing it either top center (avoid bottom right or the right edge in general as that's where the lens button will be when people click on the pin to enlarge it) or bottom center. Just remember to keep it tasteful. You don't want your logo to overpower the rest of the design. You just want it to add to it.

Easy To Read

One of the biggest mistakes I see people make on Pinterest is to over-clutter their pins or use fonts that are hard to read.

2020 and going forward, a lot of people use their phones to buy things on the internet. That means that 8 in 10 people that are on Pinterest at any given time are using a tiny screen to scroll through a whole lot of pins. So, you probably have a split second to capture someone's attention as they scroll past your pins.

If your pin doesn't stand out in the crowd or if people can't quickly read what you've written in your pin, you're missing a whole lot of opportunities to get traffic over to your business website.

It's crucial that your pins are legible, and that your text stands out. Here are a few quick ways to make sure that happens:

- Use transparent or faded out backgrounds and make sure nothing overlaps with your text.
- Make sure that your text size is big enough to be read even on a mobile screen.
- Use easy to read fonts
- Alternate your fonts to make sure words pop out.

Keep in mind that while sometimes a simple font choice is to blame for a hard-to-read pin, creating cluttered pins that have too much going on can also distract people from your headlines.

Keep your pins relatively simple, light and try to follow a given color scheme as well that should tie into your branding.

Perfect Copy

The copy of a pin, also known as the text that goes on it, can make or break your click-through rate.

Looking past the pin's aspect, the words you display on that said pin matter more when people decide to either click to read your post or scroll past it.

One of the reasons I recommend having multiple pin templates is that you get to A/B test your copy and find out what phrasing resonates more with your readers.

If you're a blogger, you probably know how much bearing a headline has on the click-through rate on your posts when you promote them on social media. We also have to consider SEO optimization, so sometimes we sacrifice a good title for a well-keyworded one.

Phrasing a blog post title in different ways when creating pins will allow you to see what your target audience responds to better and will enable you to play around with other titles, without sacrificing SEO value.

To give you a few examples of a well-written copy for pins, I had a look at the most popular pins[10] at the moment, and here are a few titles that I believe are pure genius:

- "Popular Podcasts To Listen To (Podcast Recommendations)"
- "These Will Be The 14 Most Popular Halloween Costumes This Year"
- "23 Popular Men's Hairstyles and Haircuts from Pinterest"

Can you notice any patterns in these pin headlines that led them to get more shares or clicks? At a quick glance, they all inspire curiosity, invoke strong emotion, or promise to solve a problem. Think of how you can replicate that in your pins to get your ideal blog readers' attention.

Creating your own pins can be a very time-demanding task, especially when starting out, but it's vital because the rest of this book focuses on showing you how to turn those graphics or videos into pins and use those pins to generate traffic for your business.

---

[10] https://www.pinterest.co.uk/topics/popular/

Optimizing Your Pin Descriptions

When Pinterest analyzes your account, they look at the quality of three things:

- **Your domain**. This has to do with the website linked to your account (so your business or blog) and what your own pins link to. Claiming your website and verifying it, plays a big part in earning Pinterest's trust. (All covered in Chapter 1, so if you've taken steps to verify your website and enable rich pins, there's nothing else for you to do here) I believe Pinterest views each website to see what's getting pinned from there (or what pins are linked to that website in general), and they determine the domain quality. Pinterest cares about your domain (or the URL you link to in your profile; for example, a link to your Etsy store or your YouTube). It is a fact that they prioritize content saved or created by the owner of the domain. Pins from your own website will have a more significant reach and stand a better chance in your feed, simply because you pinned them first.
- **Your pins.** To determine the quality of your domain, Pinterest takes a closer look at your pins, either the ones you create or the ones that are linked to your website. While you can't do much about what people choose to pin from your website, you have full control over the pins you create. And I'm not just talking about the pin design.
- **Your pinning activity.** Last but not least, Pinterest looks at your activity as a whole. From the boards you created (so your profile) to what you pin, how regularly you pin, and everything in between, your activity sets the tone for your success.

Now that you've created your Pinterest graphics, it is time to turn those into actual pins. This next section will give you a few pointers on why you should include your pictures in your blog posts, how to encourage other people to pin them directly off your website, how to give your pins a chance no matter who pins them, and how to optimize them to be found in Pinterest.

Develop Content Into Pins

There are two ways to turn your content, graphics, and videos you just created into pins, and I use both alternatives, depending on which is more convenient at the time. Both methods can be done via a computer or mobile phone, your choice.

Here's how you turn your content into a pin:

Uploading Them Directly Onto Pinterest

The first way is to simply upload the graphic you created (so the JPG file, for example) from your computer to Pinterest. All you have to do is go to Pinterest.com and click on the "Create Pin" button. Choose "Upload image" from the dropdown menu that appears, and drag and drop your file of choice (or click to upload it from your computer).

You will also be asked to enter the destination URL for that pin, where you will paste the link to the blog post you created the pin for and a description. You can go back and edit these at any time after adding them to a board of your choice.

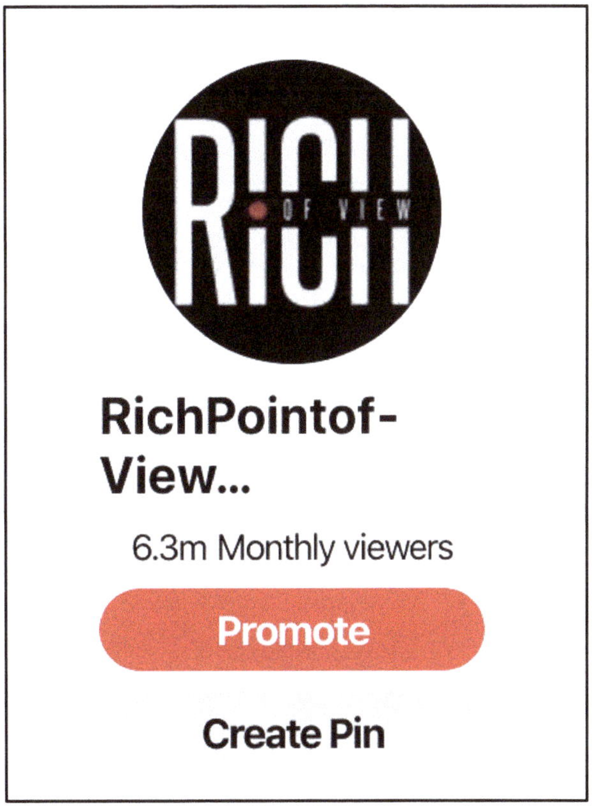

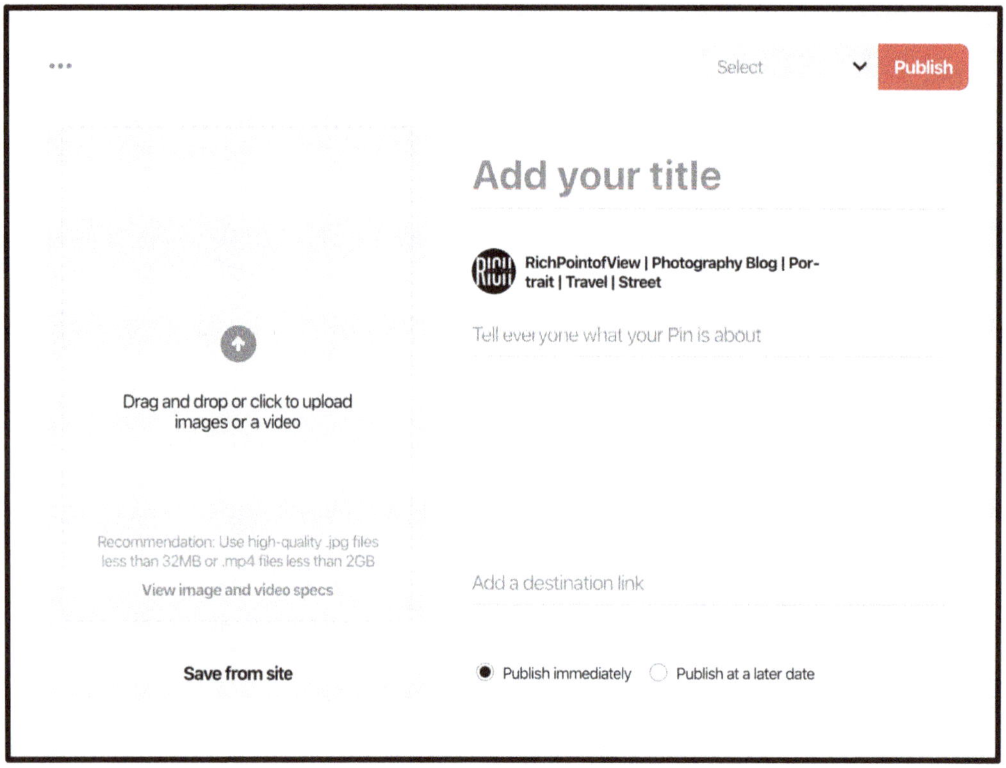

It's that simple! You can repeat the process for every graphic you have created.

Upload Them On Your Website, Then On Pinterest

Another method to create new pins for your graphics is merely uploading the picture you have developed into the relevant blog post (just like you would upload any other image) and pin it directly from there to any board of your choice.

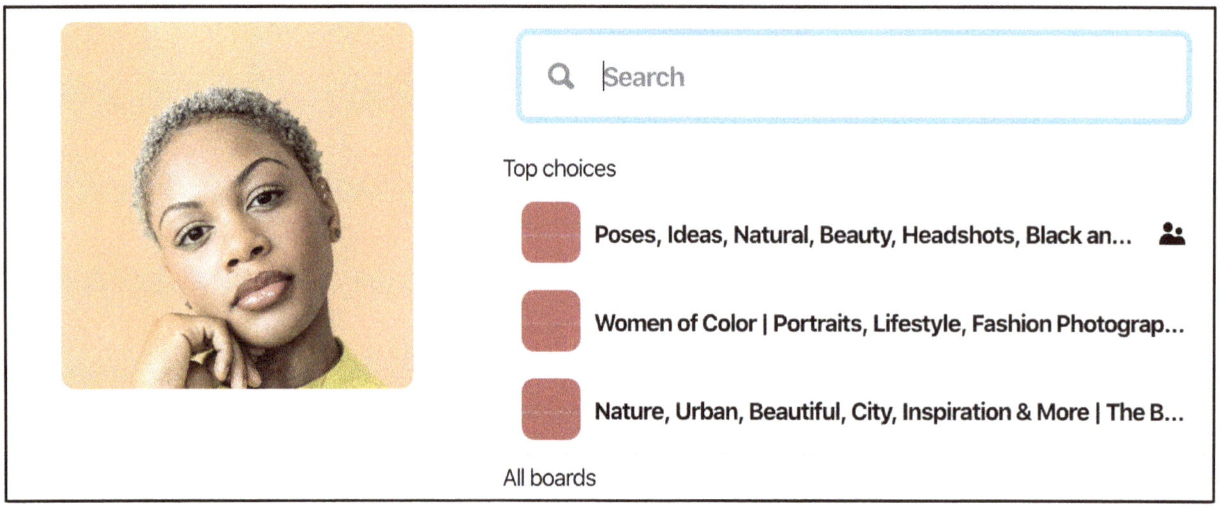

Follow the same process > hover over the image > click pin > select a board. The pin will automatically be linked to the blog post you pinned it from.

Alternatively, you can copy the URL of your blog post, click on the red upload button on Pinterest > select "Saved from the site," paste the URL and choose the relevant photo to upload to Pinterest.

I find this helpful when I've included multiple pinnable photos into a blog post because it saves time (for example, if you're a food blogger and you've included multiple photos and a graphic into a blog post, and you want to pin them all, this is the way to do it). Otherwise, to save individual pins, I just go to the actual blog post, service, or product and pin the graphic from there.

Photos In Blog Posts

Regardless of the way you choose to upload your content to Pinterest, I recommend including at least one photo within each blog post.

The main reason you should do this is that it allows your blog readers to save the article later and share it with their Pinterest followers in the process. It's free publicity.

Including a tall, vertical graphic, will make people more inclined to save that to Pinterest. Also, because the pin will be automatically linked to your blog post, service, or product, you're not only encouraging social shares, but you're also gaining an opportunity to get free traffic without doing anything! Who doesn't love free, organic traffic to their business or product?

Over the last few years, I've picked up a few tricks to encourage people to pin off my website more often and to make sure that what they pin is optimized, so that when it lands on Pinterest, it can quickly gain traction, resulting in more blog traffic for me. I do all this passively.

Here are a few best practices that you should comply with every time you add a Pinterest graphic into a blog post to maximize its efficiency:

Pin Descriptions

When people pin off your website, they rarely pause to write an insightful, keyword-rich description for the pictures they are about to pin. That usually means that those pins won't have an extensive lifespan, or won't show up in search results, because Pinterest can't really tell what they are about.

If you want to make sure that the graphics within your blog posts are optimized when they reach Pinterest, without leaving it to chance or relying on other people to do it, then all you need to do is embed a Pinterest description within your photos.

The place where you can do that is called an "ALT tag" or "Alternative Description." After you've uploaded the picture to a blog post, all you have to do is click the edit button and insert a keyword-rich description (with hashtags) in the ALT tag box. No coding or anything fancy required. This goes for people who host their websites on both WordPress & Squarespace.

Encouraging Others to Pin Your Images

With over 300 million users, it's almost impossible that your blog readers don't have a Pinterest account. Yet, some will scroll by your pin graphics without pinning it merely because it doesn't occur to them to do so.

An effortless and straightforward way to encourage more people to pin off your website is by adding a call to action before or after your Pinterest graphics, where you tell people directly what you'd like them to do.

It's incredible what a significant impact a simple sentence can have. I urge you to experiment with adding calls to actions in your blog posts, to see if your audience responds to it. Here are a few examples:

- *Pin this for later*
- *Save to Pinterest!*
- *Share this image on Pinterest.*

Optimizing Your Pins For Pinterest

Now that your pins are on Pinterest, the worst thing you could do is sit and wait for the magic to happen. As mentioned in the intro of this book, there is no magic: just strategy, hard work, and experimenting.

Whether your pins do well or not is mostly up to you. Fortunately, as someone who has seen pins flop and pins take off, I have a few things to say on the subject that might actually be of help.

Rich Pins

I've already covered this subject, but I thought I would mention it again because rich pins do offer pins extra value. Rich pins can pull data from your website, YouTube, Gumroad, etc. and tell Pinterest more about the context in which that pin can be helpful.

This helps Pinterest to distribute your pin in the right places to the right people.

I've already included a few helpful tips on how to set up your rich pins in the first chapter, but something that I haven't mentioned yet is the fact that there are 5 types of rich pins:

- **Article rich pins** (perfect for bloggers and content creators)
- **Product pins** (perfect for store owners)
- **Recipe pins** (for food bloggers)
- **App pins** (for apps)
- **Video pins (perfect for content creators)**

If you write any type of content online (blog posts, articles, etc.), then having the article rich pins enabled can be of tremendous help because, besides all the added information about the article and the author, they also come with one call to action encouraging people to "Read It."

Pro Tip: Rich pins tend to show the very top few sentences of an excerpt of your blog post if you've written one, or otherwise, they pull up the first few sentences from the blog post it's linked to. If you want to make the most of that space, make sure you write a custom excerpt (within your blogging platform), as shown below.

If you're a food blogger and want to enable the recipe rich pins, there are a few things you should consider. When enabling the recipe rich pins, Pinterest pulls the ingredients list from your website and shows a preview of it directly on Pinterest.

Rich pins also have a particular call to action under their description, inviting people to "Make it." When they click on that button, they are redirected to your post, and I believe that to be very effective in driving traffic.

This has its pros and cons. On the one hand, it allows Pinterest to dive deeper into the content you linked to, and show your recipe pins in relevant results. More than that, Pinterest can look at the type of recipe and the ingredients included and categorize your pin further.

Another benefit of having rich pins is that by having the ingredients listed on the pin and the time it takes to cook, people who come to your website to read the full recipe spend more time there because they are genuinely interested in the recipe. Perhaps they already had the ingredients they saw on Pinterest, or they were looking for something to cook quickly, and the pin gave them all that information.

Based on the information that rich pins pull from your website, pinners can sort ingredients, time, and other criteria when looking for recipes.

At the same time, most recipe bloggers fear that having their ingredients on Pinterest will stop people from clicking over to their posts, so they might be missing out on traffic.

This is a theory that I couldn't experiment with myself, because I obviously don't post recipes on my blog. I do recommend taking this into your own hands and analyzing the results.

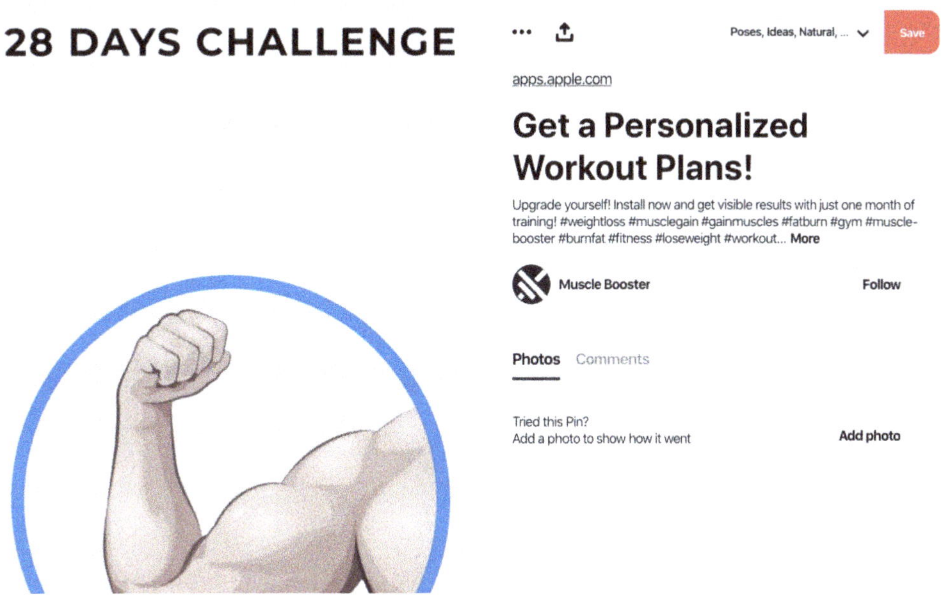

Muscle Booster uses videos to create brand awareness on Pinterest. When clicking on one of their videos, the link goes to their app download—no ad spending, just quality videos that generate clicks & downloads.

My conclusion is that Pinterest is the only platform that's incredibly generous with its traffic, and they want business owners & content creators to thrive. So, I know for a fact that rich pins have been created to help us get found.

Pin Descriptions

This is what you really want to pay attention to because it applies to you, whether you are a blogger, service provider, store owner, or online entrepreneur of any other kind.

The single most important thing that you can do to make sure your pin gets found and generates enough interest to drive a click-through is to add a well-written keyword-rich pin description to each and every single pin that you put out there (that leads back to your website/app/YouTube).

A mistake that I see many content creators make is when they stuff keywords in the description, separated by a slash or comma. (Example: fitness | ab workout | weight loss |, etc.).

While that's better than no description at all, investing your time into coming up with well researched and well-written pin descriptions are what's going to determine your Pinterest success.

Good Pinterest Descriptions

First of all, merely listing the keywords one after another doesn't work because you want your pin description to feel editorial like a real person wrote it.

If your description sounds robotic or spammy, people will assume that the content that lies on the other side is the same, and this will negatively impact your click-through rate, not to mention the SEO value of that pin.

Use actual sentences that would make sense if read out loud and sprinkle the keywords throughout in a conversational manner.

Your keywords should be specific (what that particular pin is about) and broad (the theme surrounding that pin).

Here are two questions you need to answer when writing your pin descriptions:

- What's this specific pin about?
- What are some other broader things/themes/searches that I want this pin to show up for?

For example, if you have a workout regimen pin, you want to include both the terms "weight loss" and "fitness." For a post about Instagram, you would like to have both the words "Instagram tips" and "Social media marketing."

Once you have figured out what keywords you want to use, create a few sentences around them, and you have the beginning of your description.

For the workout example, you could write something like, "For many women, achieving a lean midsection is no easy feat. Men's and women's muscles are different, etc. You can work out your body with weights or without."

In case you're struggling to come up with relevant keywords, here are two things you could try:

- **Look at the main keywords you have included in your original blog post.** There's no need to do the research twice if you've optimized your blog post for SEO already. I often just grab chunks of the introduction of my post and paste them into my description. Pinterest also puts a lot of weight into making sure that the keywords you use in the pin description correspond to the posts you're linking to, so this is accepted and encouraged.

- **Use Pinterest's guided search feature to find out what the most popular searches are.** Start with something small like "workout" and see what else pops up in the bar of suggestions on top. Only select the ones that are relevant to your posts. Then go back and search for a broader term, like "workout routine." See what else comes up there and use those to form longer and better keywords.

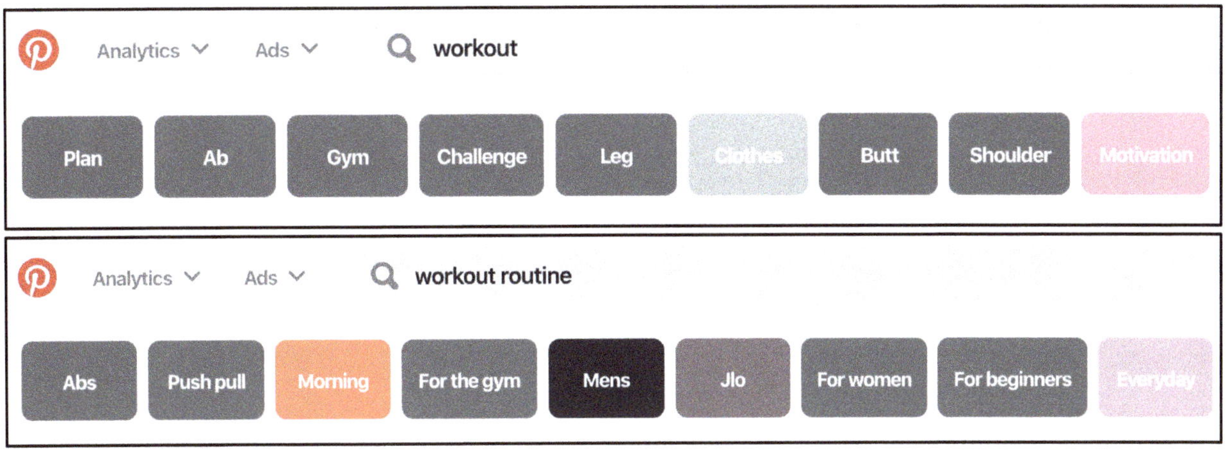

Write a different description for every pin you create, even if they led to the same blog post. To take it a step further, try changing up that description each time you repin the pin as well. This makes Pinterest look at your pin as a new pin, which is their favorite type of pin (it's worth more than a repin), and it will boost your pin's SEO value. **CHEAT CODE!!!!**

Keep in mind that you only need to do this when repinning your own pins, as it doesn't benefit you or your profile to spend time changing up the description of third-party pins.

Writing Powerful Calls to Action

A surprising fact about descriptions is that people actually read them when they click and zoom on to see your pins. In fact, pin descriptions that include a strong call to action (a direct invitation to click through to read the post) were proven to have a higher click-through rate than pins without.

Don't skip this step! It can be as simple as inviting people to click to read more. The idea is to reiterate the promise of what the blog post can offer pinners and what they can find on the click-through. Pins that do that successfully inspire curiosity by guaranteeing to provide the solution for a problem or paint the benefits of clicking over. They always provide more website traffic.

Make sure your descriptions have these two things (well-researched keywords, a powerful call to action), and you will reap the benefits.

Pinning Activity

If you bought this book to get more traffic to your business & blog, and you're already familiar with the best practices included so far, this is the part you really want to pay attention to.

You've set up your profile, you've created pins, and you've optimized them. Now it all comes down to distributing them.

How Often Should You Pin?

Let me clarify the myth that there is a certain magic number of pins per day that works for everyone. There isn't.

I started with a blog post a day, roughly around 30 pins per day, and slowly added more while keeping a close eye to see if my Pinterest traffic was increasing, stagnating, or decreasing. (You want to give it at least 2-3 weeks to really be able to tell, before making any changes.)

Now I'm at 60-70 pins per day. I tried going higher, but my traffic didn't improve, and I wanted to be more intentional about what I pin as well. So, I found a sweet spot in the middle, and even now, I try to experiment with it and change it up.

There's no universally correct answer. For sure, whether you choose to pin 30 or 80 pins per day, you need to make sure that:

1. You're consistent
2. You're spreading your pins throughout the whole day/week

You should start out by testing some products or a blog post a day. Track your analytics and increase as time goes on. Be intentional with what you are posting, and there shouldn't be any issue.

Is There A Such Thing As Pinning Too Much?

Pinterest came out to confirm that you cannot pin too much. They love active users and want to reward them, so you won't be penalized if you pin over a certain number of pins per day.

On the other hand, I have heard and read about a few people getting banned on the platform. Is this from pinning too much or them having spam content, I have no clue? I was forbidden from pinning for 3 days at one point in time last year. I emailed Pinterest, and within 72 hours, I was able to pin again but was never given a formal explanation as to why.

In my opinion, the only facts you need to consider are the following:

- **You need to be considerate of the user experience that your followers get.** Due to the smart feed, even if you pin 20 pins per hour, Pinterest will pick and choose which ones to display. To avoid spamming your followers, I would spread my pins equally during the day and the week, and not pin more than 20-30 per one sitting or the same image more than twice in a row.
- **You need to be mindful of where your pins go.** When you pin too much, you get less time to spend on each of your pins, and that's not always wise. The reason I chose to pin less, rather than more, is so I can better optimize my own pins.

What Should You Pin?

This is a straightforward yet complex question. When it comes to the content you can pin, there are 2 types of pins to choose from:

- Your own pins - created and pinned by you- lead to your own website/blog (affiliate links are an exception, but they still count as your own pins).
- Third-party pins - pins created by other content creators/pinners- lead to other people's blog posts/websites.

Should you be pinning more of your own pins, or third-party pins? The answer is just as frustrating as before: there is no magic ratio as I continue to say. Every account is different.

If you decide to pin 30-80 pins per day, and you have at least 300-400 original pins of your own (and you come up with fresh content and pins regularly as well as me), then there is no need to ever pin other people's pins because you can rotate your own without overlapping them and spamming your followers.

The only time I personally use third-party pins is when I am starting a new board. I do this to bring traction to the board itself, and then I start adding my own pins that I created.

If you are just starting out, or you're not creating new content regularly, then sharing third party content comes in handy, because:

- **It breaks up your own pins so that they don't overlap.** By pinning third-party content, you get to pin the same image to a board multiple times, or various images to the same board, because of how you space your pins, so you don't come across as spammy. If the group boards you are in do not allow identical pins or have a cap on how many pins you can add per day, make sure you respect that rule.
- **It helps you curate content for your audience** on topics you might not necessarily blog about (but that are in the same niche), and this will increase the chances of you getting followed because your profile will be a go-to place for that topic.
- **It gives your boards more context and enforces the keywords** you're trying to build up around them.

Where Can You Find Third Party Pins?

If you're wondering where you can find relevant third-party content to share that would interest your readers and be relevant to your niche, here are a few ideas:

- Use the smart feed (the homepage of Pinterest that you land on) to see pins recommended by Pinterest, based on your activity.
- Use the search function of Pinterest to find anything and search by hashtags to find recently posted pins in your niche.
- Take a look at the group boards you're a part of and share from there.
- Pin directly from the websites you visit that are in your field.

How Much of Your Own Content Should You Share?

While third-party content has all these benefits and can be really helpful when you only have 30 pins of your own or are just starting out, people get sidetracked by them and forget that their real focus needs to be on their own pins.

With that in mind, I discovered that once you have over 50-150 pins of your own, you can increase the ration of your own pins, so that you pin more of your own content than you do of someone else's.

Being a photographer, I have access to an enormous amount of content at my disposal. I'm sure food bloggers, fitness gurus, etc. have that luxury as well.

Before I reached close to 1,000 original pins of my own, I was already pinning 60% of my own content and 40% of third-party content, and I think that was one of the reasons why my account took off and I started seeing a spike in traffic coming from Pinterest, even with a small following. At this point in my Pinterest journey, 100% of pins that I post are my own, varying from blog content, products, and services.

The whole reason why you're on Pinterest is to promote yourself and your business. That's not selfish. If Pinterest sees no benefit in sharing someone else's content, it's because they want you to get your own content seen, and let other people worry about themselves.

Which Pins Are The Best?

In Pinterest's eyes, new pins and repins have entirely different values.

This offers us precious insight into what pins Pinterest is more likely to pay attention to, show to our followers, and recommend to others. By paying attention to the "fresh pins" rule, we can guarantee a more significant distribution and reach for our pins without paying for them.

Now that you know how precious fresh pins are, allow me to explain what they actually are, and paint a picture of the best type of pins, in order:

- **New pins for brand new articles/blog posts are the best.** Pinterest loves fresh content, so when you create a new graphic for a blog post you just published, and add that to Pinterest, you are hitting the jackpot! (And because you claimed your website, you bring in organic traffic to it.) This applies to products & services as well!
- **New pins for older blog posts.** The next type of fresh pins that Pinterest adores (but not as much as the first type) is new pins and graphics for old blog posts. So if you have a few older posts that you updated and that you want to get some more traffic to, create some new Pinterest graphics for them and add them to Pinterest.
- **Same old repins.** Repins count the least in Pinterest's eyes, especially when we are talking about sharing your own content. That doesn't mean they don't matter - because they do count as engagement (it's dope as hell when other people repin your pins, for example), and they help your content spread beyond your reach. When it comes to sharing your own content, going directly to your website to pin a graphic matters more because that is seen as a new pin, rather than a repin, especially if you add a unique description.

Is Manual Pinning Best?

As I've already said countless times, everyone has a different Pinterest strategy because not everything works for everyone.

As long as you are pinning, logging into your account each month, and creating new pins, Pinterest considers you active.

I DO NOT USE TAILWIND!!!!!!! Ok, let's move on.

It's evident that based on your possibilities and the time you can dedicate to growing your Pinterest, you get to choose whether you would manually pin or automate, or even combine the two. That doesn't matter in the grand scheme of things, as long as you follow the right Pinterest strategy.

So, if you have the time to pin each day and keep track of everything - do that like me. If you'd rather not worry about it so much, and save some time in the process, get a scheduler.

For the past year or so, I've pinned manually directly from my phone. This process has worked for me tremendously. This strategy may or may not work for you.

Regardless, I highly recommend starting to implement these tips for your own accounts (whether you choose to do it manually, or automate it):

- Be intentional about what you pin
- Reshare your own pins from the smart feed
- Reshare your pins from the notification tab

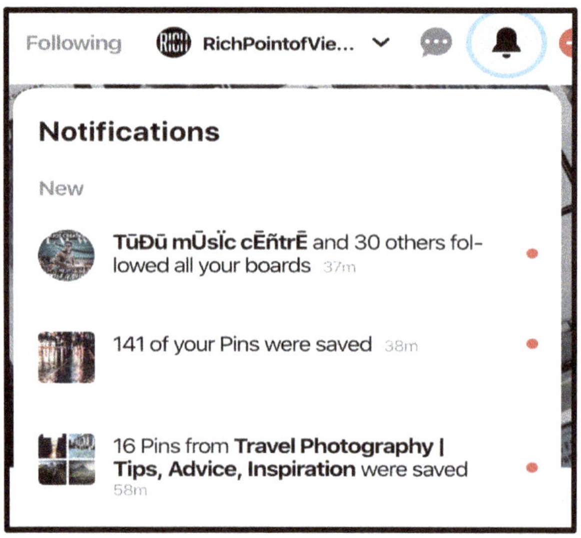

Tracking Your Progress & Understanding Pinterest Analytics

I hope this chapter will clarify what these numbers mean, where to find them, and how to better understand them to tackle weaknesses and inspire you to keep moving forward when you see some progress.

As you try these new strategies, it's crucial to understand how they impact your account and traffic, but you need to give it time (and ideally not stress over the numbers or take them personally).

Reading Your Pinterest Analytics

Pinterest does a decent job of telling us how our account is doing. (To get access to these insights, you will need to have a business account and claim your website, as shown in the first chapter.)

Your Pinterest analytics are separated into 3 categories:

- Profile analytics
- People you reach
- Website analytics

You can see an overview of all three by going to Analytics > Overview in the top left corner, right next to the Pinterest logo.

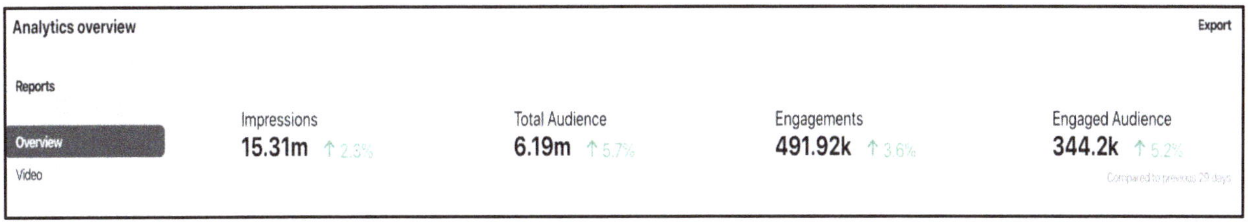

Below, is a full screenshot of the various analytics you can view in the analytics section.

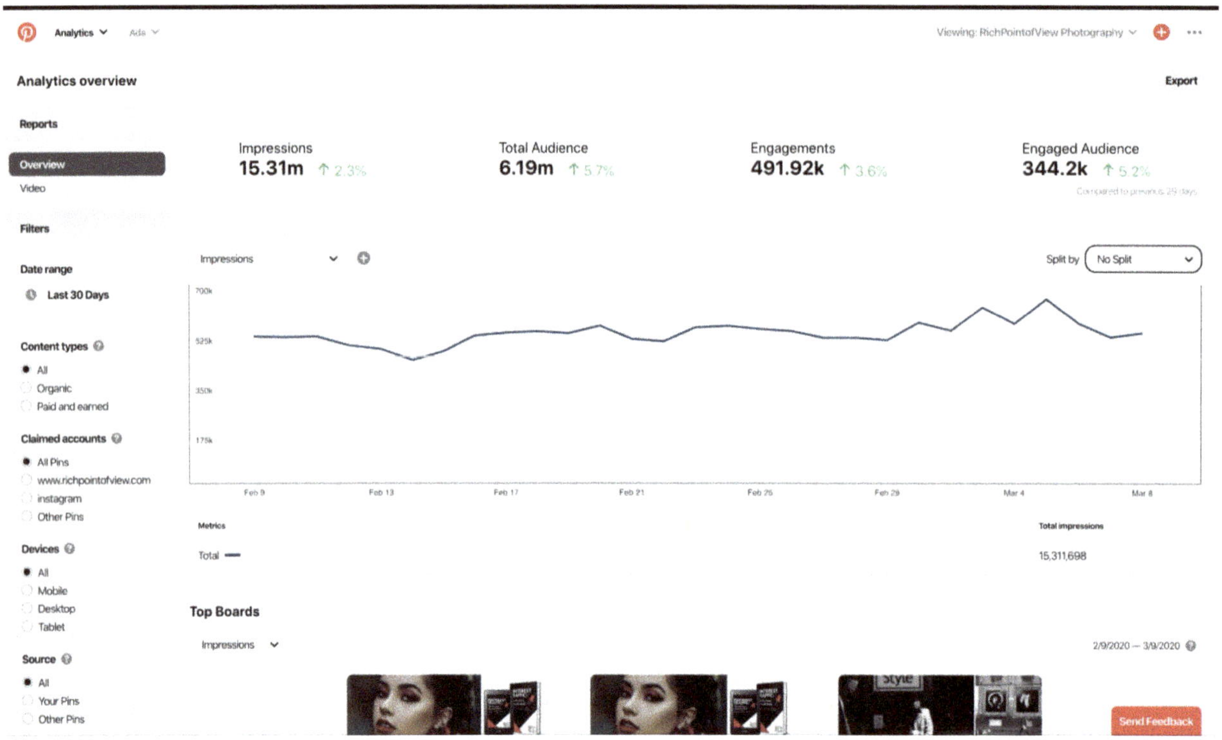

Growing Your Pinterest Following

If you do everything that I've talked about in the book so far, your account will grow itself. Even when I put the least amount of time and effort into my account, Pinterest was still my fastest-growing platform yet.

I reached 10k followers without much effort - just regular pinning, good profile SEO, and a follow button on my blog.

While doing that, I've picked up a few unspoken Pinterest secrets that I'll share in this chapter. Consider these tips a roadmap to your first 10k Pinterest followers.

Do Follower Counts Matter On Pinterest?

Pinterest is more of a search engine than a social media platform; therefore, followers don't matter (at least, not as much as they count on other platforms).

That is because Pinterest allows you to expand your reach well beyond who chooses to hit the follow button, and with all the new ways to get your content discovered, it's wiser to focus more on your pins and implement a good strategy.

The recent change - to display your monthly viewers bigger than your follower number on your profile - is a conceptual change that Pinterest did to encourage pinners to focus on producing quality content and increasing their reach, rather than just their followers' number.

They want you to understand the potential your content has to be seen if you use their platform correctly, and I hope this book will help you do that.

But still, it's foolish to believe that followers don't matter at all, especially with the constant Pinterest updates. Here's why:

- By introducing the **following tab** that people are beginning to spend more and more time on, they want users to be able to see content from people and accounts they've curated, and the following tab does that.
- **Pinterest displays your content to your followers first**, and based on how they interact with it, they are more or less likely to index it for search and distribute it further.

Let me break that down: you create a new piece of content and pin it. Pinterest shows this pin to a majority of your existing followers. If the pin gets good engagement (close-ups, re-pins, clicks, comments, or anything else), they distribute it further to people who don't follow you yet, search results, and so on.

If the pin gets low engagement from your followers, they limit the pin's distribution until they get proof that people are interested in that content.

So, quality followers matter. Numbers matter as well to some degree, but they shouldn't be your priority. If you have 15k followers, you have 15 times more chances to get your content seen by your followers than accounts with only 1k followers.

At the same time, it's better to have 1k followers that are going to engage with your content and are interested in what you pin, then to have 15k followers who never interact with your pins.

As you're continuing to read this book, really think about ways to apply my tips and strategies in a way that reaches your target audience. This is a vital way to gain organic traffic.

You can make slight changes to my tactics that will help you reach the people who matter, and if you can't, simply skip that step.

I find that most of these tips can be universally applied, because you get your profile in front of more people and, usually, only the ones that love what they see hit the follow button.

Quick note, in case you're hoping to gain 15k overnight: that's not possible. Took me over a year to get there. It was hard work and a lot of patience, so this book is now coming out after a year of grinding and implementing various strategies.

Here are some tactics that I used to grow my account to 15k followers:

1. Be Active

The first one is straightforward. You need to be on Pinterest, pinning, interacting with pins, and other users. You should do so frequently.

You can't be the ideal Pinterest user for a week and then desert your account for two. This is why I started out pinning a blog or something from my portfolio daily.

Pinterest considers your account active if you are continually adding new pins (so both manually pinning and automating your account count as being active) and log in from time to time.

I also believe that Pinterest loves when we act like real users from time to time. I think that these little actions made a big difference in my growth:

- Interact with other pins and clicking through to other websites.
- Interacting with other pinners.
- Pinning from my phone when I have free time

If you've converted from your personal account to a business account or haven't really been paying attention to who you've been following, it's the best time to do a spring clean of your following list.

Once every 3-6 months, I go in and unfollow inactive accounts as well. This is only a personal preference, but my follower growth really accelerated once I cleared up my list.

2. Get Your Readers & Consumers to Follow You

This is one of those universal rules that will apply no matter who your audience is because guess what? Your audience hangs out on your blog.

A very simple way to find people interested in your Pinterest content is to look for people who love your content first, which are your consumers.

If you have social buttons on your blog, you're probably already doing this and driving traffic to your Pinterest account. Now, let's take it a step further.

There are a few ways in which you can make sure that people who visit your blog, visit, and follow your Pinterest profile as well:

- **Add a pop-up on your website.** Many bloggers ask blog visitors to follow them on Pinterest in a pop-up, as soon as they land on their blog. I've definitely seen it work firsthand.
- **Add a call to action in your posts.** Every time I mention Pinterest in one of my blog posts, I also include an invitation to come over and follow my account. If my post is on a topic that I have a board on, I link to that particular board instead, as a way to invite people to discover more personally curated content about a topic they are clearly interested in. Think about ways to introduce a little call to action within your blog posts to help readers discover your Pinterest account.

3. Social Media Presence

As you started your blog or business, you chose to focus on other social media platforms as well. If that's the case, and you have gathered an audience outside of Pinterest, why not take advantage of your influence to direct people towards Pinterest?

Promoting your Pinterest account on other platforms is a great way to make sure that your target audience knows about your account and follows there too. Cross-platform promotion is one of the easiest things to do these days.

Facebook groups for bloggers are another great way to get the news out there, not only about your Pinterest account but also about your blog or service-based business in general.

These groups have designated promotional threads that allow you to promote your blog, special offers, or social media accounts within the comments.

4. Create Your Own Group Boards

When people hear about group boards' power, they underestimate how this power can be multiplied when you're the actual owner of such boards.

When I started my account, I had some trouble finding group boards on more specific topics such as "Social Media Marketing" or "Photography," so I decided to go ahead and create my own.

I now have over 4 group boards of my own on several different topics, and my biggest board has approximately 200 contributors.

Want to know why I invested so much time into creating, promoting, and managing these boards? Let me give you a rundown of the benefits of having your own group boards:

- **My pins get a better reach on my own boards.** As you can imagine, these boards are highly active, but they are also receiving a lot of engagement. Pinterest loves boards with a lot of third-party content (other people's pins) which means that whenever I add a pin of my own in my Photography group board, it gets a much bigger reach then it would if I would've added it to my personal board (or even some of the group boards that I'm a part of that have a bigger following).
- **It helped me grow my email list and boost my affiliate income.** At the end of the form that people had to fill out to receive an invite, I invited people to check some of my photography related blog posts or products & services. I already knew that people were trying to grow their photography reach, so by offering them freebies or tools that they can use to do so, I actually got some unexpected benefits. Depending on the type of boards you own, you can do the same.

From my own experience, creating your own group boards has a significant impact on your reach and on raising brand awareness at the same time. I definitely recommend starting at least 2 or 3 group boards of your own and testing this theory.

5. Refresh Your Boards & Groups

Something else that you can try, and that can help your pins perform better, is to create and join new boards from time to time.

You can never have too many boards (or group boards) and brainstorm a few more boards that you can create or join.

Every time I publish a new post and realize I don’t have a board on that sub-topic, I create it. Simple, yet effective.

If you haven't done it in a while, go and create a few more boards or request to join some new group boards this week. The closer they are to your niche and topic, the better for you in the long run.

6. Promote Your Pins (Optional)

Once your pins are already getting good engagement and traffic, you can take it a step further and pay to expand your reach.

This is not something that I do often (because Pinterest already offers us such unique opportunities to reach people), but a little boost can really help a pin take off, and pinners who tried it swear by the fact that pins continue to do well, even after they stopped promoting them.

The only time I would personally use this tactic is to sell a product, service, or want to gain more traffic to a landing page for an increase in conversion rates.

If you're considering promoting your pins, everything you need to know is included in this free Pinterest Ads guide[11].

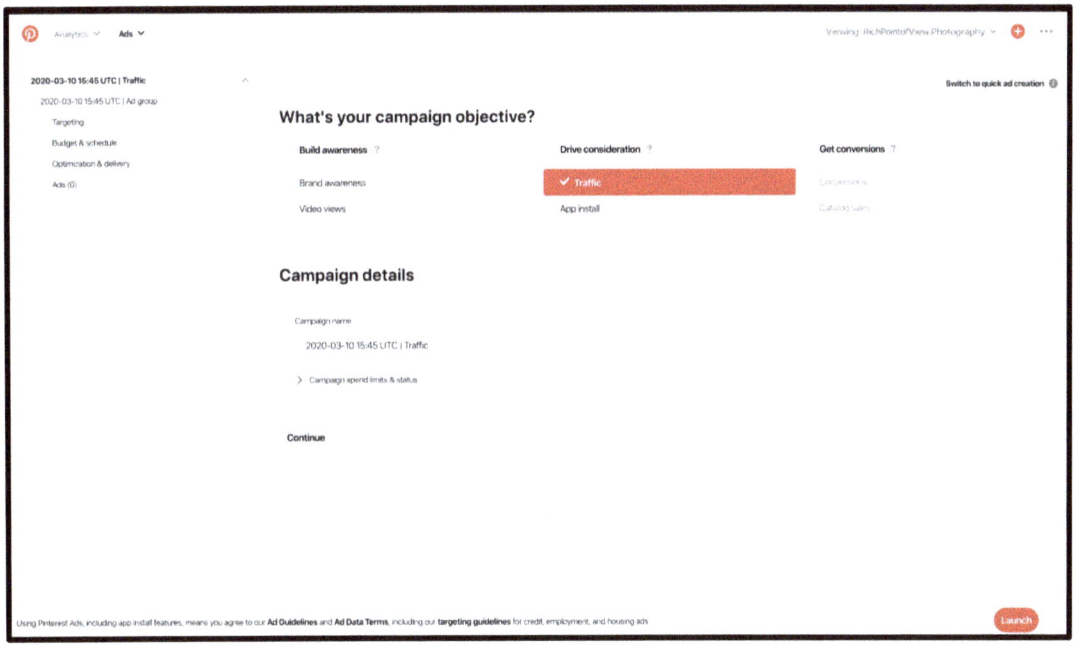

Give it a try and see if it works for your account too.

[11] https://business.pinterest.com/en/using-ads-manager?utm_medium=2023&utm_source=31&utm_campaign=738bfb&utm_term=2018-05-21

7. Post Fresh Pins

We already know by now that Pinterest loves new pins, and a way to consistently be on their right side is to always create unique content. What I haven't gotten around to discussing is that there is a peak time when you really want to put all your effort into making as much new content as possible, and that is when Pinterest is going through an update.

Throughout your Pinterest journey, you will notice that your stats are sometimes not influenced by what you do and that you won't be able to control the rollercoaster. Remember, this is **ORGANIC TRAFFIC**, don't sweat it!

If you've already analyzed your activity, and you can't figure out what's causing a drop in views or a sudden improvement, the answer could simply be that Pinterest is going through an update.

As your journey progresses, keep in mind that followers matter, but the quality of those followers matters much more.

There are reasons why the Pinterest hack is covered in 9 chapters, while followers are only discussed in 1.... that's because you should always have your focus on optimizing your profile and your pins, rather than on your followers.

Pinterest Business Resources

Pinterest is optimized for brands because Pinterest users love to discover new products and businesses on the platform, so Pinterest makes it easy for companies to promote their products and brand.

Pinterest provides plenty of great resources to optimize your Pinterest marketing strategy and get the most out of your Pinterest business accounts.

- Pinterest Trend Predictions[12]: An annual trend report that unveils its predictions of the top trends of the year. Checkout what Pinterest has labeled as trending for the year and going forward.
- Pinterest Webinars[13]: The latest and greatest in Pinterest research, directly from Pinterest themselves. Examine these webinars to get the most out of your Pinterest business account.

---

[12] https://newsroom.pinterest.com/en/post/pinterest-100-the-top-trends-to-inspire-and-try-in-2020

[13] https://business.pinterest.com/en-gb/webinars

- Pinterest Success Stories[14]: Many companies use Pinterest for business as part of their overall marketing strategy, and you can learn more about what they do and their results from these case studies provided.

Conclusion

Congratulations! You made it to the last chapter without going crazy, **AND** you learned a new social media tool to take over for your business!

As an ending note to this book, I just want to encourage you to stick with Pinterest, even if it seems like you're doing a lot of work for little or no reward.

If there's anything you should take out of this book (other than some practical tactics that you can start implementing today), is the fact that there is no magic formula to success and no one way to do it right.

This book is based a lot on my own experience and what has worked for me. While I'm proud of my Pinterest results, I'll say it once again: every account is different, so every strategy should be different. **TEST. IMPLEMENT. PIVOT.**

Last Words

I have poured a lot of time, effort, and expertise into this book in the hopes that it will make a difference in your business growth and equip you to use Pinterest with purpose.

The world needs more of your content, your services, and your products. Please, get excited to share it.

If there's anything I missed, or if you have any questions at all about the contents of this book or about Pinterest in general, please email me at richard@richpointofview.com. I am more than happy to be of further service.

If you follow the strategies outlined here and get results that you're proud of, reach out to me, and I can add case studies to this book as time goes on.

Thank you once again for supporting me and my business by picking up a copy of this book. It really means a lot! **LET'S GET IT!!!**

---

[14] https://business.pinterest.com/en/success-stories

Lastly, if you just want to share this book with your friends, family, or blog readers, why not join my affiliate program and get 35% of each sale you refer to? Be sure to email me at richard@richpoinotofview.com to get your referral code!

BONUS CONTENT

Steps to Advertising on Pinterest

Why Use Pinterest Ads?

Pinterest is an excellent social media tool, with over 300 million users ready to consume. It enables the discovery of information through images. The unbranded searches through Pinterest are one way to grab a future client's attention in a subtle way, which leads the pinners to be more open to new ideas and products.

98% of pinners say they've tried new things that they found on Pinterest, versus 71% found on other social media platforms. More than half of Pinterest's users have made a purchase after seeing business content on the site. Compared to non-pinners, they deliver an average of $2 more in profit for every advertising dollar.

Types of Pinterest Ads

We will be going over six different types of Pinterest ads. This will help you determine which will better suit your company and what kind of advertising you are trying to mandate through Pinterest.

Promoted Pins

Promoted pins appear in the home feed and in search results, just like a regular pin would. Other than being labeled as promoted, they look and behave the same as any standard pin. They're boosted and targeted to deliver a higher reach. Once a user pins them to boards, shares them, or comments them, the "promoted" label will go away. This is considered earned media, giving you exposure for free. When the pinner taps or clicks your ad, they're taken directly to your landing page.

Promoted Carousels

People use Pinterest for inspiration and unique discoveries. That's precisely why this is such an excellent option for any business, especially when trying to showcase different products or features. Promoted carousels behave the same as regular pins but have the opportunity to use a multi-image ad that can feature additional images, titles, descriptions, and landing pages for each photo. This is great for reaching out to different types of pinners to highlight the many facets of your products or brand all within one single pin.

Promoted Video Pins

Promoted video is just like promoted pins where they appear in the home feed, search results, and the "more like this" section. Videos are ideal for bringing awareness to and tell the story of the brand or product. The videos will autoplay as soon as they're 50% in view, without audio. It is essential to create content that is not relying on the audio, but the actual imagery since most people watch videos with the sound off. It's available in standard width and max-width formats, which spans out into two columns on mobile devices, giving you a higher chance of being sought after over competing pins. Videos are four times more memorable than non-video ads, according to a study conducted by Millward Brown for Pinterest. 67% percent of pinners say that videos inspire them to take action. If you are looking to boost traffic, conversions, or increase performance goals, videos would be an excellent place to start.

Promoted App Pins

If you're promoting an app, this is the BEST way to do it. It allows pinners to download the mobile app directly from Pinterest. Just make sure you are highlighting your app's attributes through your promotion. This is a good fit for a Pinterest audience, especially because 80% of their traffic comes from mobile devices. These promoted app pins look and act the same as a promoted pin or promoted video pin, but includes an install button that links directly to a valid iTunes or Google Play app store URL. Pinners are already looking to consume, by looking for inspiration and ways to make their lives easier, so a quick and easy download can turn into a sale for you.

Buyable Pins

Buyable pins are a way to sell your products right off the bat without trying to engage a pinner to go to your site. These pins allow consumers to find and buy products directly through the photo itself. The best situation would be to have a staged aesthetically pleasing photo, including the items you're trying to promote. The items are then tagged in the image being promoted with white dots that can be tapped or clicked to link to product information. It will also include a blue button that says "add to bag." These buyable pins are designed to maximize sales. Modern Citizen, the fashion brand, saw its retail orders increase by 73% after using buyable pins on Pinterest.

Story Pins

This is a new form of advertising on Pinterest. A lot of apps are playing around with stories. Story pins can feature up to twenty pages of images, texts, and links. This story pin will appear on the home feed with a cover image and a title. When tapping a story pin, it allows you to see all of the pages. They can also be saved to boards just like a regular pin.

How to Advertise on Pinterest

Now that you're familiar with all the ad formats, you're now ready to start advertising on Pinterest. Here are the 13 easy steps to promote on Pinterest.

Step 1: Get a Business Account

This is probably the most effortless task. You can take your existing Pinterest account and convert it to a business account by going to your account settings. You also have the option of creating a whole new Pinterest account and setting it up the same way.

Step 2: Install the Pinterest Tag

The promoted tag will give you access to track the actions people are taking on your website after seeing your Pinterest ads. This includes checkouts, sign-ups, and searches. You don't want to skip this step before creating your campaign.

Step 3: Choose your Campaign Goal

This will determine what ad formats are available and how you bid in the ad auction. After you choose your goal, head over to ads.pinterest.com[15].

Here are the available objectives:

- Grow your website traffic: Earn high-quality leads that you will pay for with each click.
- Build brand awareness: Gain exposure to current and prospective clients. You will get charged per 1,000 impressions.
- Downloads for your app: If you pay by install, Pinterest will adjust your bid based on your personal budget. If you pay by the click, your ad is optimized for click traffic.
- Awareness through video views: Promoted video pins are created to get people to take charge and to considerable promote their products or services. You will pay per 1,000 impressions.

[15] https://ads.pinterest.com/

Step 4: Campaign Budget

Here is where you will put your name to your campaign and set your daily and lifetime spending limits. There will be more pricing options, later on. So, don't spend too much time worrying about this section. Make sure to enable this option if you're creating a carousel ad campaign. This will only work if your campaign objective is brand awareness.

Step 5: Create an Ad Group

Ad groups are for managing multiple goals within a single campaign, while still maintaining lifetime spend caps at your campaign level. You can assign budgets and targets to ad groups. You should have about two to four pins per ad group.

Step 6: Choose Your Target Audience

Based on the product you're trying to sell, the app you're trying to promote, or the website you're trying to generate traffic for, you will need to know your target audience based on gender, location, language, and devices used. If you're looking to just specifically spread awareness, use a broader targeting strategy to generate a higher click volume.

Step 7: Select Ad Placement

If you have a higher budget, go with all the default placements. If not, there are two options, browse or search. Browse placements end up in the home feed and related pins of interest targeting. Search result placements perform better with keyword targeting.

Step 8: Add Interests and Keywords

Using interests and keywords on your ad campaigns will help reach the correct audience as they search for a specific idea on Pinterest. Use keywords related to the ad you're promoting and use negative keywords to exclude the wrong pinners. For the best results, it is best to use at least 25 keywords per ad.

There are five different ways you can use keywords to your benefit.

- Broad match: Pins show for your own keywords, it doesn't matter the order they are in.
- Phrase match: Pins show on search terms that include the same search term phrase in order of the keywords.
- Exact match: Pins show based on the exact keyword. The word order matters.

- Negative phrase match: Your pins will not show on any search that contains the entire keyword phrase in the search term. The word order matters.
- Negative exact match: Your pins will not show on a search that matches the keyword exactly. The word order matters.

Step 9: Set Your Budget and Schedule

This part is essential as it cannot be changed once saved. Here is where you can enter your start and end date for your Pinterest ad campaign, as well as the lifetime budget or daily spending limit. The lifetime budget is how much you want to spend in total from start to end. The daily budget sets the spending limit for your ad group.

Step 10: Tailor for Optimization and Delivery

Minimum bids must be above $2. Set your maximum bid for your Pinterest ads for your target CPM rate. The total price paid in a CPM deal is calculated by multiplying the CPM rate by the number of CPM units. Example: one million impressions at $10 CPM equals a $10,000 total price.

Step 11: Determine Your Pacing

Standard pacing and accelerated pacing are the two options you will have. Standard pacing is probably the best option if you want your ad to last through your campaign end date because accelerated pacing may drain your budget. For high impact campaigns or a crunch, accelerated pacing can be a good option because it will yield fast delivery and results.

Step 12: Pick Your Promoted Pins

Each ad group should include two to four pins. Here is where you will click a pin to add pins to your ad group. You can create new ones or pick pins you've added before. They cannot be saved to secret boards or third-party feature videos. They must be saved to your profile and include a destination URL that has not been shortened.

Step 13: Monitor Campaign Performance

To keep track of your campaign's performance, you can go to the Analytics from the Pinterest Ads Manager dashboard. Here is where you will find an overview of all your campaigns along with the performance details for each. Make sure you are broadening your audience, increasing your budget, and trying different formats to optimize results.

If you have any questions related to advertising on Pinterest or any feedback, it would be great to hear your thoughts via Twitter[16] or email[17]!

[16] https://twitter.com/RichPointofView

[17] richard@richpointofview.com

Powerful Conversion Ideas for Entrepreneurs & Ecommerce Stores

According to one study, a majority of e-commerce stores only experience a conversion rate of around 3%. If this low conversion rate reflects your situation, it probably means that you're getting a short ROI with the money and time you are spending to increase your website traffic. Building traffic through CPC, PPC, social media, or SEO can be beneficial but are only part of the puzzle when we're talking about increasing conversion rates.

Pinterest + Your Lead Magnet Increase Conversions

Those of us who have learned about Pinterest know that it attracts people who are - or soon will be - consumers once they come to engage with our products & services.

Pinterest is an excellent tool for helping people learn about products, prices, research competitors and gain clarity about what they want.

Purchases can happen when a motivated buyer finds a pin that leads him or her to a product page on your website.

It is a passive way to easily make money but it is highly unlikely for someone to find what they want and purchase immediately.

The more likely scenario is that they come to Pinterest to do some extensive searching.

Prospects click and save a few pins that are interesting to them and return the next day, maybe a week or two, depending on how vital the need is and how busy their life is. We've all been there.

Business Grows When You Engage Your Audience

Most likely, by doing so, you have them in your funnel. Now you can send consumers emails sharing valuable information and getting them excited about your upcoming products & services.

This strategy gives you an advantage over the other pins they may have saved. If this occurs numerous times, you will see a sizeable increase in cash flow and profits.

Do you realize how important having a sales funnel and providing a lead magnet can be?

If you are like many service-based businesses or e-commerce stores, you should already have a functioning sales funnel to capture leads for future marketing efforts. If not, let's take a look at using a lead magnet in a funnel that can operate in expanding your store and getting repeat sales from customers.

Assuming you're using Pinterest as a lead magnet generator, imagine you were the only service-based business in the pins they saved who offered them a lead magnet (aka "freebie") to gain their email address.

What Exactly Is A Lead Magnet?

The sole purpose of a lead magnet is to offer a high-value incentive for website visitors and prospects to get a free item in exchange for their contact information (most likely their email address).

It's essential to create lead magnets that attract the right prospects and convert them to be a part of your mailing list. Now, you can imagine how important it is to get to know and understand your target audience so you can give them the information they consider valuable.

You are most likely looking for their email address to keep in contact with them, but some types of companies may also look to obtain a phone number or a link to their social media.

Here are 5 key action steps in most cases:

1. Create your lead magnet.
2. Offer the lead magnet on your website.
3. Website visitors decide they want your free lead magnet offer and agree to provide their name and email address.
4. The lead magnet is downloaded or obtained by your potential customer.
5. They are now part of your email list and can receive relevant and targeted emails based on their needs and wants.

Why Do You Need Lead Magnets?

The use of automated emails is the most effective strategy to increase your sales in the world of internet marketing. But first, you have to build an email list.

To build an email list, you must have a sales funnel and exceptional lead magnets to get your potential consumers inside the funnel. Trust me. There's no better way to drive traffic leads to your website than start with a Pinterest pin and a captivating lead magnet.

Starting out, you must show that you're credible and actually promoting and selling products that are useful to your audience. Your lead magnet represents how you conduct business and how well you know your niche. If the audience thinks it will benefit their lives, they will share their email.

Afterward, you have various opportunities to make your case. Remember, they need your product or services.

What Are The Characteristics Of Lead Magnets That Convert Into Sales?

- Given its purpose, your lead magnet needs to guarantee that it's beneficial to your target audience. Consumers will assume you don't know or care about them if your free lead magnet offer isn't interesting or doesn't offer any value.
- It should solve a specific problem that your prospects have that is important to them.
- It should drive immediate action. Your lead magnet should provide a tool or information your potential customers desire and can apply immediately.
- An effective lead magnet makes lives better or easier.
- It should be ready for adoption immediately. People love getting instant pleasure, and your potential customers are no exception. Deliver your lead magnet as quickly as possible, usually directly.
- Most great lead magnets are free. Your email list will grow to become highly targeted and responsive if your lead magnet fits into their lives.

Lead Magnets That Can Boost Conversions

Here is a list of lead magnet ideas and how you can use them in a funnel for your website + Pinterest traction. Only use the examples you believe will provide a benefit for your target customer. When executed, they give them a reason to start trusting you and share their email address.

1. Coupon

Coupons are the most utilized lead magnet for an eCommerce site. Let's be clear upfront - you are definitely asking them to make a purchase.

Using this strategy, you may see less than a few people taking advantage of a "freebie" offer. Coupons are primarily used for a discount on a purchase, but can also offer a freebie of sorts.

Why do coupons work so well? It's easy to use and offers value to your potential customers. Plus, they'll have to make a purchase from your store to take advantage of the coupon.

You should know that not all offers are compelling for your potential customers. Sometimes, even if you feel like the deal is a generous one, your potential customers may not see it that way.

For some reason, if the discounted product isn't top-rated, your offer may actually fail and not motivate visitors to subscribe to your mailing list, which you don't want.

2. Quiz/Survey

Quizzes usually have a high engagement rate.

You simply have your website visitors answer a series of questions and then ask for their email addresses to send their results.

Generally, it's best to ask for their email address after they've answered because by then, they most likely want to see the results.

Furthermore, it's best to tailor the quiz to your product niche and what you're selling on your website.

These types of quizzes can also have a prize for the winner or winners.

3. Checklist

Checklists are tasks compiled and summarized into a single list. They can be easily made, downloaded, and read. Many bloggers & entrepreneurs like them for that reason.

Think about using checklists as lead magnets in your eCommerce store as well. For example, if you're selling wireless chargers, you can provide a checklist of allowed and prohibited substances under the TSA guidelines.

4.Tutorial

A tutorial is a piece of content that teaches how to perform a specific process. The most successful tutorials come in the form of an infographic, a PDF document, or even a video tutorial, which is most common.

Even when running an eCommerce site, your tutorials shouldn't be strictly limited to products. Think about teaching a process that uses one of the products you sell. A tutorial is an excellent choice if you want to feature a product (preferably your most expensive one or bestseller).

For example, if you sell fitness equipment, you can offer a short video tutorial on how to correctly adjust settings and ways to use the product for different benefits. Of course, the fitness equipment will be from your product listings.

I like to repurpose a previously written "how-to" blog post about an essential process in my niche and turn it into a tutorial.

5. Offer Daily Deals

The advantage of being an entrepreneur or owning a business is that you can offer a deal any day on any product or service you choose.

Turning your promotional deals into lead magnets is key. Make them too good to pass up. By doing so, visitors will want to give you their contact information to receive updates on your amazing daily deals.

6. Offer discounted & free shipping

Free shipping can produce a pool of customers loyal to your e-commerce store, as shipping costs are one of the few expenses that online shoppers would rather not incur. Shipping costs can also attribute to empty carts and having potential customers leaving your website without a purchase.

You surely won't be alone in offering this lead magnet, but unlike other companies, perhaps think of sending them a free 2-3 day shipping code for any purchase over $50+.

A minimum order amount for using the code will not be a surprise as many online retailers choose this route.

7. Email Course

The email course is a series of emails sent in a strategic order that discusses an important topic with your audience over a specific time.

If you feel a tutorial might give away too much information in a single delivery, you might want to consider serializing it to an email course. This way, your prospects can get bite-sized details per email.

8. Ongoing Drawing for a Valuable Giveaway

Unlike a freebie offer, giveaways are won by a few lucky candidates.

Therefore, a giveaway needs to be a product (or combination of products) with a higher value than what you would give as freebies.

To influence the right people to engage with your giveaway, you must present the right product or service for giveaway. Nothing's better than using one of your own products or services. Or, you can consider a bundle of related items that can be presented in a giveaway.

Don't go with something your target audience doesn't relate to in your product line. If you do this, you boost the odds of getting individuals to sign up who could care less about your products.

I've discovered through my own process that giveaways work best if they're done regularly. This is dependent on your product area, but once per month usually works ok. Potential consumers will be more likely to stay on your list, so they don't miss out on winning the next giveaway.

This offers an excellent possibility for some social media exposure.

Encourage the winners of your giveaways to post about it on social media with the use of a hashtag that correlates with your brand. Social proof helps verify that there are, in fact, real winners in your giveaways. The visibility alone should motivate other interested audiences to subscribe to your email list.

Lead Magnets and Pinterest Work Together to Jumpstart Sales

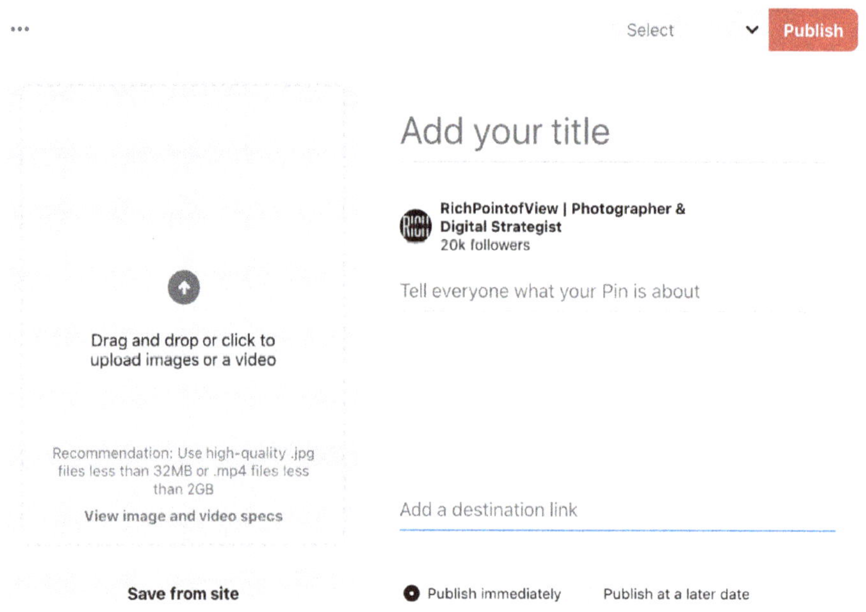

ALL LEAD MAGNETS HAVE A URL!!!! You should have MULTIPLE options created in Canva for your lead magnets, and all you have to do is upload them to Pinterest!!!! IT'S THAT EASY!!!!

Lead magnets are crucial to building a mailing list and developing a customer base that trusts your experience and the quality of your goods.

Pinterest marketing to drive potential customers to your lead magnet and tripwire or follow-up funnel will increase conversions and help you, your services, and e-commerce store to rake in higher profits.

MAKE SURE YOUR URL IS ON THE WEBSITE YOU CLAIM FOR YOUR BUSINESS ON PINTEREST OR IT WILL SHOW UP AS SPAM!!!!

Affiliate Marketing: Making Money on Pinterest

Making Extra Income On Pinterest With Affiliate Marketing!

So here's the central business idea:

For the inexperienced, Pinterest[18] is a visual search engine. Customers search for inspiration and 'pin' images that they love to come back to later. Every 'pin' is an image with a link attached to it. Consumers can click on the image to visit the site it came from.

We can monetize this with **affiliate marketing**.

So what's affiliate marketing now?

"Affiliate marketing" is solely promoting an item online and getting a commission for any sales. You promote the product using your own unique tracking link, which is called an **affiliate link**.

Anyone who clicks on your link and buys a product, the seller can see that you referred them, and you get a portion of the sale!

There are numerous ways to promote your affiliate links and make online sales.

The most common tactic is blogging. You can share your links on social media, or directly to your email list.

Why it's Natural to make money on Pinterest!

Consumers go to Pinterest to look for inspiration, and curiously **look for things to buy, whether now or in the future**!

Recently, a statistic showed that 87% of users[19] have bought something they found on Pinterest, and an astonishing 93%[20] say they've used Pinterest to plan future purchases.

This means it's smooth and straightforward to promote exceptional products on Pinterest without looking spammy.

---

[18] https://www.pinterest.co.uk/boostmybudget/boards/
[19] https://blog.hootsuite.com/pinterest-statistics-for-business/
[20] https://blog.hootsuite.com/pinterest-statistics-for-business/

Your pins on Pinterest have a very long shelf life, unlike Twitter, where your message disappears from the timeline just hours after you tweet.
When a pin gets picked up and gets a lot of repins (shares), it will show up in people's feeds without any effort.

You need to have at least a blog or website to make money on Pinterest. Anyone can create a Pinterest account and start pinning affiliate links.

You don't need hundreds of followers, either.

Again, Pinterest is a visual search engine. This means that if you pin nice looking images with useful, keyword-rich descriptions, your niche will find it – no matter if they follow you or not.

Is affiliate marketing on Pinterest legal?

Mixed information about affiliate links on Pinterest has floated around for some time. That's because they were forbidden for a period thanks to abuse by spammers. However, since May 2016, they're officially allowed again[21].

Now, you shouldn't abuse the system, and you should try not to come across as a spammy user.

Here are some fundamental guidelines for staying legit on Pinterest:

- Using misleading images or descriptions to trick people into clicking on your links is forbidden
- Flooding Pinterest with hundreds of affiliate pins without repinning other content is frowned upon
- Always follow the rules & guidelines if you are invited to any group boards.

Be sure to view Pinterest's community guidelines[22] for more information.

If you are adhering to rules, there's no reason NOT to use affiliate links on Pinterest.

Done correctly, you are only helping people find the products or information that they came to Pinterest for.

So, how can you get started?

---

[21] https://business.pinterest.com/en/blog/affiliate-links-are-now-allowed-on-pinterest
[22] https://policy.pinterest.com/en/community-guidelines

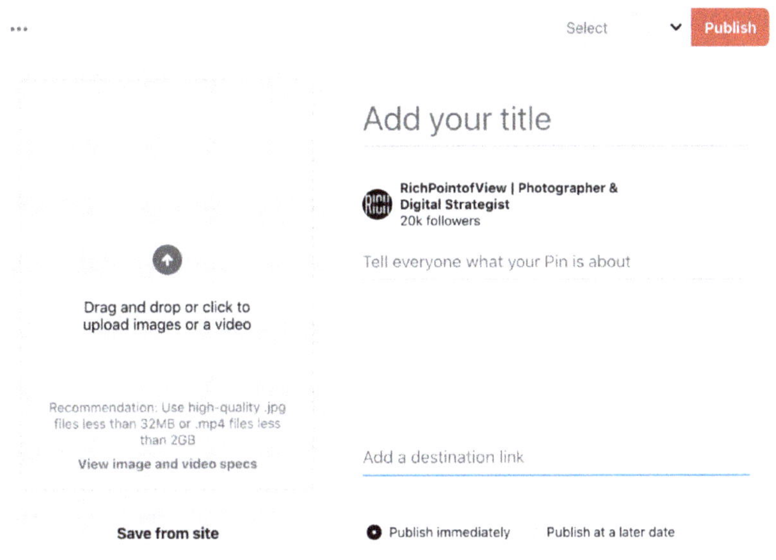

Walkthrough to making money on Pinterest with affiliate marketing

1. Make A Pinterest Account

To start, you obviously need a Pinterest account! If you've read through the book already, you will know all about this and its significance.

Already have a personal Pinterest account? You should start with that. You don't need a particular account for affiliate sales.

It's a huge benefit if you already have an established account with some followers, just like any other online platform.

Having a Pinterest business account just gives you extra features like statistics and analytics that are helpful.

If you've made a new Pinterest account for this, you'll want to start filling your boards so that they can at least start getting traction. I recommend starting with 3-5 boards on topics that are interesting to you and/or that you want to promote products in. This could be anything from clothes to electronics to fitness products!

You can find ideas of trending topics here[23], but really, anything you can find an affiliate link for works.

[23] https://trends.pinterest.com/?country=US

After you've done your research, pin at least 15-20 pins to each board. Don't bother worrying about affiliate marketing at this point. Focus on repinning other people's pins to fill out your profile.

2. Sign Up For Your Favorite Affiliate Programs

Now that you have a Pinterest profile up and running, you'll need to find profitable products to pin – from businesses that will pay you!

There are tons of different companies & entrepreneurs that pay commission to affiliates for promotion.

The majority of large retailers you can think of have their own affiliate programs.

One affiliate program I highly recommend for general Pinterest marketing is called MagicLinks[24]. MagicLinks is dope because it covers thousands of different retailers under one program literally, meaning you don't have to waste time applying to various affiliate programs individually.

Through MagicLinks, you can create affiliate links from numerous products in categories such as electronics to arts and crafts, pets, weddings, books, food, and anything in between.

It is required to have a minimum of 100 Pinterest followers to join MagicLinks if that will be your sole promotion method, so work on building up your profile first if you're new to Pinterest.

You can also use Gumroad[25] affiliate products (something I do myself) to generate extra income.

I've created a thread on Twitter, which included a list of alternatives for Google Adsense other affiliate programs to promote on Pinterest or on your blog/website. Click here to jump there now[26].

Now, that you've set up your Pinterest profile, and joined some affiliate programs, start pinning links of the products you want to promote using the images provided.

You can use the image from the company's website or use Canva[27] to make unique pins with text overlays and other animations.

---

[24] https://www.magiclinks.com/
[25] https://gumroad.com/
[26] https://twitter.com/RichPointofView/status/1256587672803516416
[27] https://www.canva.com/

3. Make Sure That the Link Associated With the Pin Is Your Affiliate Link from the Provider

This is crucial in the process! Without this, you won't get the credit nor paid if someone purchases the product that you pinned.

Here's a step by step on how to add your pin and affiliate link to Pinterest:

Click on the red 'plus' symbol in the top right corner of your Pinterest homepage. Afterward, select 'create pin' from the drop-down menu.

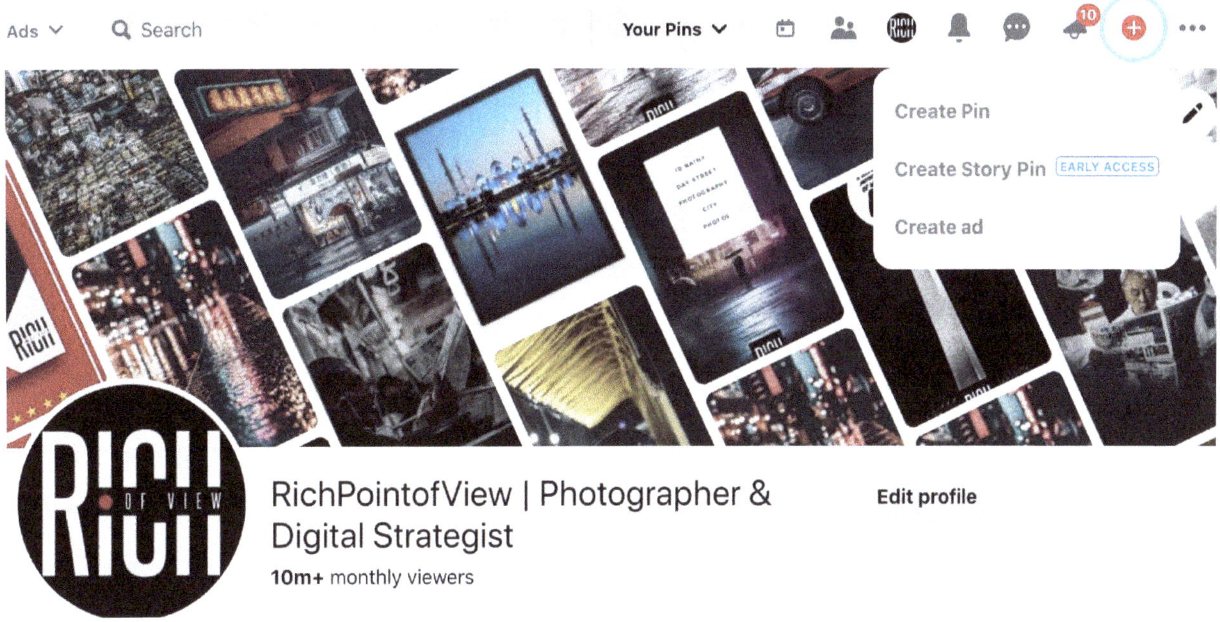

The following will show up on the screen. Here, upload your pin image to the block on the left-hand side. Grab your affiliate link from the website, and add your affiliate link to where it says 'add a destination link' at the bottom.

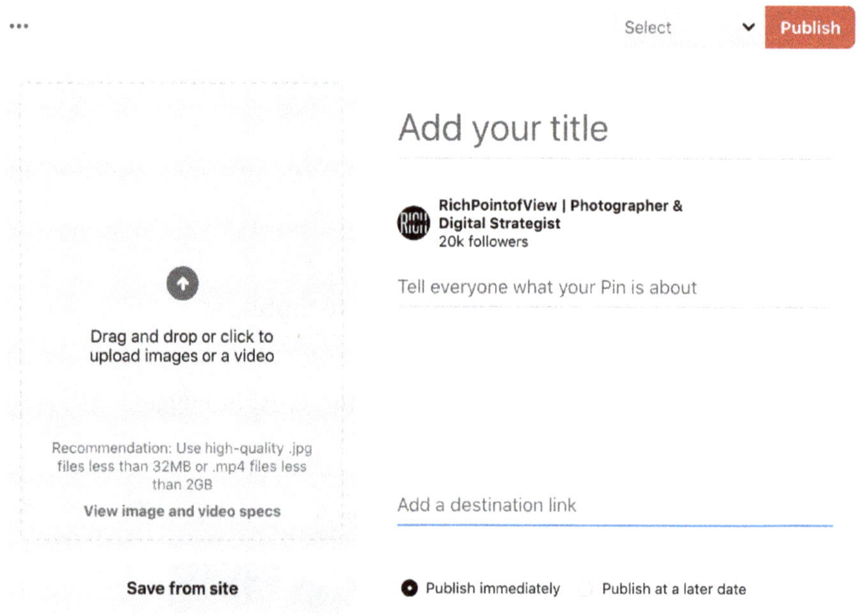

Always make sure to use the full, raw form of the affiliate link. Avoid link shorteners such as bit.ly. Pinterest itself has advised that because shortened links don't always track correctly, which means you could miss commissions.

Also, DO NOT post affiliate links via mobile app. The reason is that once you add the destination link, it clicks through to the destination and will change the link, not giving you credit in the long run if someone makes a purchase! I found this out the hard way. Rich did that, so you don't have to go through that!

Be sure to write a beneficial description for each pin.

When adding new pins, there is space for you to add a description. This is where you'll write a detailed description of your product.

4. Remember, Pinterest is a Visual Search Engine.

Use plenty of 'keywords' – the kind of keywords that people search for. This will direct people to your pin, even if they don't follow you.

You can find Pinterest's recommended keywords by studying the suggested search terms that drop down when you start typing in the search box for ideas.

As a reminder, do a Pinterest search for your primary term and look at the suggestions that pop up in the colored boxes underneath the search bar.

A quick hint: if you click on one of those colored boxes, you will get even more keywords.

So, if I want to pin some diecast cars to my stationary board, a suitable description would be something like: *"These custom cars would be great accessories & decorations for a kid's room interior!"*

This way, my will pin show up in search results of people searching for those words.

Your description will always need to include a disclosure such as "affiliate link" or "#ad."

Regulators, specifically the FTC[28] in the US and the ASA[29] in the UK require an affiliate disclosure. Always make sure that you're in compliance with the local authorities so that you're following all the guidelines.

5. Pin A Lot!

Pinterest likes people who pin a lot!

They especially like it when you repin popular pins.

Repinning other people's popular pins will keep your profile fresh and exciting for your followers. Also, it means that Pinterest will most likely show your pins more often in other people's similar feeds.

Pinterest rewards people who share popular stuff because they know you're sharing things that people want.

The more you repin popular pins, the more people will see your original & affiliate pins, which will result in more clicks!

You should try to pin a minimum of 15-20 a day. Keep in mind that not every pin will make you money in the beginning.

It isn't wise to expect a random pin to turn into a cash cow overnight.

---

[28] https://www.ftc.gov/tips-advice/business-center/guidance/ftcs-endorsement-guides-what-people-are-asking
[29] https://www.asa.org.uk/advice-online/affiliate-marketing.html

It is crucial to share *new* affiliate pins every day (preferably multiple pins!) and experiment with new pin designs, and ultimately, you will see the affiliate royalties rolling in.

The best affiliate programs to use on Pinterest IMO!

A vetted list of companies worth joining to use affiliate links on Pinterest.

Magic Links[30] – highly recommended by many. No website required. Instant access to affiliate links from thousands of shops!

ShareASale[31] – a significant affiliate network that doesn't require a blog. There are thousands of various retailers to choose from. Unlike MagicLinks, you have to apply to each retailer separately. Still, you can search for 'auto-approval' merchants to speed things up. T&Cs may vary by retailer.

Ultimate Bundles[32] – a fantastic online company that sells themed 'bundles' of electronic resources (ebooks, online courses, printables, etc.) at unbelievable discounts! They cover all kinds of topics, from interior design to online business to essential oils. Some packages come out once a year, and some are evergreen. You can promote these affiliate links on Pinterest without a blog.

Kit[33] – this isn't an affiliate program. It's a brilliant way to create collections or round-ups of your favorite products. It can kind of function like a blog in itself if you don't want to make your own website, but you want more of a platform online! You can create a collection of Amazon products on Kit, then create a pin linking to your kit. This is one of the various ways to get around the ban on Amazon links on Pinterest.

Zazzle[34] – unique gift ideas such as T-shirts, tote bags, and stationery.

How does one find more affiliate programs to join?

Additionally, to the numerous affiliate networks listed above, tons of online retailers have their own affiliate programs, which can be found on Google.

Companies will usually have a page on their website about how to join.

---

30 https://www.magiclinks.com/
31 https://www.shareasale.com/
32 https://ultimatebundles.com/
33 https://kit.co/
34 https://www.zazzle.com/

Alternatively, you can reach their marketing department via email or social media.

I suggest brainstorming the stores or products you would like to promote, and then just Google "product name" "affiliate" to see what shows up in Google.

What are the best affiliate programs to promote on Pinterest?

There's no correct answer to this question. Always do your research when looking for the best affiliate program for yourself and your niche.

Affiliates like to look for the highest paying affiliate programs and promote those, but if your audience doesn't care about that product, you won't make any sales.

I highly advise looking at what pins are performing well for you so you can make an educated decision moving forward.

Make sure to track your analytics to visualize what kinds of products and images are getting the most repins. Afterward, you can search for affiliate programs to promote more of those products.

The best thing for you to do is trial and error. Sign up for 1 or 2 affiliate programs and test out different things to make sure you are on the right path. More sales should indicate you are doing something right.

Golden rules

There's tons of information in this write-up, but here are the key points to remember:

- Don't spam
- Write great pin descriptions. Use keywords!
- Declare your affiliate links
- Repin other people's stuff
- Repin popular content
- Always show consistency
- Never give up – pin lots, and allow time for new pins to take off!

NOTES

CPSIA information can be obtained
at www.ICGtesting.com
Printed in the USA
LVHW012338291120
672987LV00014B/956

9 781734 285659